HEIST

THE ODDBALL CREW BEHIND THE $17 MILLION LOOMIS FARGO THEFT

JEFF DIAMANT

Published by Sourcebooks, Inc.
P.O. Box 4410, Naperville, Illinois 60567-4410
(630) 961-3900
Fax: (630) 961-2168
www.sourcebooks.com

Originally published in 2002 in the United States of America by John F. Blair, Publisher.

Library of Congress Cataloging-in-Publication Data

Diamant, Jeff.
 Heist : the oddball crew behind the $17 million Loomis Fargo theft / Jeff Diamant.
   pages cm
 Revised edition of the author's Heist! 2002.
 (trade paper : alk. paper) 1. Larceny—North Carolina—Charlotte. 2. Loomis, Fargo & Co. 3. Criminal investigation—North Carolina—Charlotte. I. Title.
 HV6661.N82.D5 2015
 364.16'20975676—dc23
                           015006077

Printed and bound in the United States of America.
VP 10 9 8 7 6 5 4 3 2 1

Contents

Au_____'s Note

In 1997, I was a reporter o_____ beat at the *Charlotte Observer*, just a few years out of _____ group of North Carolinians who didn't think thi_____ 17 million from an armored-car firm called Loo_____ When they were arrested in 1998 and their jaw-d_____ revealed, I assumed I'd never see anything quite like it a____ this point in my career, that's been true.

Not that it's been slow for me. Since then I've covered many other fascinating stories, often of national and international significance—the presidential election recount of 2000, the aftermath of 9/11, and the papal funeral and subsequent conclave of 2005, among other things. Unlike those events, the heist, it is safe to say, will never be mentioned in a history textbook. Yet thanks to the foolishness associated with it, and the compelling stories of the people involved, it has a special spot in the memories of Carolinians who followed it in the late 1990s. That's especially true for the journalists who covered it.

⊰⊱

As the lead reporter on the case for the largest newspaper in the state, I was able to develop sources that helped me tell the most complete story possible at the time. Facing stiff competition from local media, especially the *Gaston Gazette*, as well as national publications and news shows that occasionally came to town, I was the first to secure in-depth interviews with most of the defendants in prison or at their homes, as well as with the law-enforcement agents who explained their investigative process in detail. Most of the important information gleaned from individual interviews was corroborated through interviews with others, and on the infrequent occasions when accounts differed, I resolved matters through available court documents and further interviews. My work paid off with enough information to fill a four-part series in the *Charlotte Observer* that was later republished in the *Washington Post*. This book is the product of many, many more hours of work.

Public interest in the heist has never disappeared. The latest cable documentary appeared on MSNBC in 2014, and now, in 2015, Hollywood is in on it. It's easy to understand the staying power; this is a captivating tale of greed, broken dreams, and things gone wondrously wrong, a tale that spurs readers, between guffaws and eye rolls, to place themselves in the characters' shoes and consider how they might have acted differently. I hope you enjoy it.

Inside the Vault

"Don't double-cross us," the woman on the phone told David Ghantt. "Don't back out on us. Steve's a serious guy."

David didn't appreciate her tone. Who was *she* to be pressuring *him*? *Steve* was a serious guy? It was David who was hours away from committing the most daring act of his life, and she was going off about *Steve* being a serious guy?

He angrily hung up the phone at Loomis, Fargo & Co., his soon-to-be former employer in Charlotte, North Carolina. It was 2:00 p.m. on October 4, 1997, and tension was building between two planners of what would rank high among the largest heists in United States history.

The woman on the phone was Kelly Jane Campbell, and David had a mad crush on her. She had attitude. Spunk. A parrot tattoo on her right ankle. She was five-foot-seven, had dirty-blond hair, and had worked with him for about a year at Loomis Fargo, until she left for another job in 1996. But they'd stayed in touch, and now they were poised to attempt a crime like almost no other.

After hanging up on her, David returned to work. The only other employee with him on this day was a trainee. David was supposed to be showing him the ropes of the job, which included cash pickups and deliveries. Loomis Fargo, the nation's largest privately held armored-car company, used vans to transport hundreds of millions of dollars a day belonging to banks and other businesses, stocking automated teller machines and storing money in the Loomis vault between deliveries.

The trainee didn't yet know how the place worked, a fact David planned to use to his advantage. At 2:20 p.m., the phone rang; it was Kelly again. "Everything's gonna be all right," she told him. The plan was still on, but David remained steamed. "Just remind Steve," he said, "that I might be trouble my *own* self." Getting that off his chest calmed him some, and the conversation returned to the plan.

David said he needed Kelly to drive to Loomis before the theft that night to remove a duffel bag from his parked pickup truck. The bag held his mobile phone and handgun. He added that he would be able to send the trainee home at about 6:00 p.m. and would then need about an hour to load the money from carts, shelves, and the floor into a Loomis company van.

"Do you know how much there's gonna be?" she asked.

"About fourteen or fifteen million dollars," he said.

When they hung up, she called his pager and left the code 1-4-3, beeper-speak for "I love you," based on the number of letters in each word.

Kelly had approached David with the idea in the summer, knowing he had a crush on her and winning him over with the promise that a shady friend of hers with Mafia ties would help them. The friend was Steve Chambers, and Kelly said he knew his way around the world of crime. David and Steve had never met, but Steve had already secured somebody else's birth certificate and social security card for him and given it to Kelly to pass along. David and Kelly had driven to Rock Hill, South Carolina, and used the documents to obtain a fake ID that David would also rely on after the theft.

The reason David didn't know Steve's last name was so they couldn't identify each other to the police or FBI, should cops or G-men ever enter the picture. These weren't the hardest of criminals, and though there was logic to not knowing each other's names, they had derived some of their methods from Hollywood depictions of crime. In *Reservoir Dogs*, released just five years earlier, the pawns in a robbery knew each other only by assigned colors: Mr. Pink, Mr. Blue, Mr. Orange, Mr. Blonde.

The actual crime itself required none of Hollywood's imagination. David would simply empty the vault and deliver the money to the others. The loot would later be divided among David, Kelly, and Steve. David's share would be sent to Mexico, where he planned to hide and where he expected Kelly to join him.

David's vision for all of this actually derived more from books than from movies. As a child, he had preferred reading to playing sports, and he would say, as an adult, that although he couldn't have told you "who was on first," he knew as a kid who the Egyptian god of the dead was. As an adult, he preferred

Shakespeare, Tom Clancy, and any book he could find about the Federal Bureau of Investigation.

In fact, he had recently finished a book about the FBI and felt it provided insight into the agency's investigative techniques, insight he thought could help the little gang succeed. This was several years before the advent of smartphones and the post-9/11 increase in federal surveillance of electronic communications, and public knowledge about this tracking was less widespread. David told Kelly they would have to control themselves and not spend the money too quickly, because the FBI could electronically trace a suspect's recent spending activity through bank papers, credit card records, and land transactions.

"For the first year after a crime," he told her, "they're all over you, with six to ten agents. But after a year, they cut it down to two agents. And after two years, the case is just a file. If we can sit on the money for a year, maybe two, it could work."

That was taking the long view. A more immediate need was securing help to move the stolen money to safety the night of the crime. David knew this was important from having followed the recent news about a Florida man who had brazenly committed the biggest heist from an armored-car company in United States history, a loner named Philip Noel Johnson, who also had worked for Loomis.

Johnson had stolen $18.8 million earlier in the year, on March 19, 1997, only to be caught five months later, in late August, while crossing into Texas from Mexico to retrieve some of the money, which he'd hidden in a shed in mountainous western North Carolina. A customs inspector, asking routine questions of bus passengers, focused her attention on him when his answers reminded her of Tommy Flanagan, the pathological-liar character played by Jon Lovitz on *Saturday Night Live*.

Asked the purpose of his visit, Johnson had replied, "To visit friends."

The guard asked, "To visit friends?"

Johnson said, "Yeah, that's it. To visit friends."

In David's eyes, Johnson's big mistake was that he did it alone. Learning from this error, David planned to leave the stolen money behind with his coconspirators while he fled to Mexico. He would then have the bulk of his share sent south of the border. If it didn't work out, he could return to the United States later with a new identity.

David placed their odds of success at 85 percent, a confidence inspired by faith not just in his planning but also in his feelings for Kelly. He wanted to leave his wife for her, and Kelly, who also was married, let him think she wanted the same. The stated plan was for her to move to Mexico to be with him after the theft. They hadn't slept together or even fooled around much, but he was ready to commit. Their only intimate physical contact had been kissing on a mid-September night when they had driven her pickup truck to a field behind a shooting range in Gaston County to discuss their plans and the theft's chance of success.

At that point, Kelly and David had known each other for two years. They had met in December 1995 on one of her first days at Loomis. He had approached her inside the chain-link fence that surrounded the building and said with a flirty smile, "If you give me a cigarette, I'll be your friend."

"I don't need any more friends," she'd shot back. "But you can still have a cigarette."

David got a kick out of her. They could talk about anything, even topics he couldn't discuss with his wife. NASCAR. Four-wheeling. How he felt shorted by life. How he and his wife had trouble communicating. And Kelly thought he was funny.

Except for the kiss in the pickup truck a few weeks before the heist, Kelly had kept things platonic. She'd left Loomis in November 1996 to take a job elsewhere as a security guard. Afterward, she and David would talk just occasionally on the phone. Their most important conversation occurred one afternoon in August 1997 after Kelly paged him at work. After discussing his job, his marriage, and his everyday struggles, they joked about Loomis and about how easy it would be to steal from the place.

Conversations about stealing from the company weren't rare for Loomis employees. For people earning $8.15 an hour—David's salary—the jokes came naturally. But this time on the phone, Kelly wasn't joking.

"Just think about it," she said. "What would it take to make you do it?"

Over the next two weeks, David thought about it. Living with his wife, Tammy, in a mobile home, he had longed for the middle-class lifestyle of his childhood that had come to seem luxurious, a pipe dream for him now. Growing up, David's family went to Disney World, sent him to religious school, and shopped at places he couldn't afford as a self-supporting adult. In his youth, his mother had taken him to Sears and

JCPenney, but as a man he shopped at Walmart, and while he knew there was nothing wrong with that, he wished he could afford more.

He even had to watch what he bought at the grocery store. He and Tammy could have one or two meals each week that he really liked, but the rest were hot dogs or Hamburger Helper. He was on a budget for clothes, even for work boots; he had recently needed to check seven stores before finding a pair in his price range. The Charlotte area's economy was booming all around him, and he felt passed over.

It all seemed unfair. He was a hard worker, smart enough, and had graduated from high school. He had joined the army and earned an honorable discharge, but because of defense-industry cutbacks he hadn't been able to find a good job for himself. Lacking a college degree, he found that his army skills felt meaningless in the 1990s job market.

He had since held one low-paying job after another. After marrying Tammy in 1992, he worked fueling airplanes at the airport in Hilton Head, South Carolina. In 1994, they moved to Gastonia, North Carolina, where they had grown up, and David took a job driving a forklift. Later that year, he saw a newspaper ad for a job at Loomis Fargo. He put on his best pair of jeans, a button-down shirt, and his nicest cowboy boots. The supervisor liked him and gave him the job.

In Gastonia, David would run into high-school classmates who had never struck him as especially smart. Yet their lives seemed far easier and better than his. He couldn't understand the gap, why he wasn't more successful, why he couldn't at least match the financial stability of his father, who earned a comfortable salary driving a truck.

If the American Dream involved being better off as adults than your parents were, David was experiencing a version of the American Nightmare. The unfairness gnawed at him, stirred by Kelly's questions. He deserved better. Stealing from Loomis Fargo could make him rich, if he got away with it. He could even be famous, perhaps joining the ranks of legendary master thieves.

Of course, this would all be a radical departure for him, and thoughts of his wife and parents did give him pause. He knew it would mean leaving Tammy. He knew his mother would be traumatized, shocked, and appalled. Growing up, David had been a nice kid, a decent student who was at worst a minor troublemaker and prankster.

About the worst he had done as a teenager was stealing a construction company's Porta-Jon with a friend, tying it to the back of a pickup truck, and driving around for about fifteen minutes. Then they returned it. Another time, the day after a Christmas in the late 1980s, David and some friends planted all the discarded Christmas trees from the area in one neighbor's front yard. If a prank seemed dangerous, David backed out. When some friends stole a stop sign from a busy intersection, David made them put it back.

But with Kelly's new idea on the table, several dark realities converged on him. He hated his job and his bosses, he'd lost hope in his marriage, he wasn't going to advance at Loomis, and he couldn't afford to quit to enroll in college. He realized his life wouldn't improve unless he did something drastic.

He waffled on the heist idea three or four times from late

August to mid-September. Then one day, while reviewing his and Tammy's credit card bill, he did some quick math and realized that even if they met the minimum monthly payments, the bill would take thirty years to pay. Thirty years! And they could barely afford the minimum payments, given the power bills, phone bills, car insurance bills, and home payments they had to meet. He decided at that moment that if Kelly called again, he would go for it.

Sure enough, she called a few days later, around September 16. "What would it take to convince you to do it?" she asked again.

"I'll need help moving the money, getting a new ID, and leaving the country," he told her.

"Are you serious?" She sounded incredulous.

He said he was.

"I've got a friend," she said, "who can hook you up with a new ID."

⋇

The October 4 shift was lasting longer than expected, due to delays involving pickups and deliveries. As it neared its end, David stealthily left the vault door ajar. The trainee didn't know to check to make sure it was closed.

David and the trainee left the warehouse. In the parking lot, David sat in his pickup truck smoking a cigarette and waving good-bye as the trainee drove home. At about 6:40 p.m., he went back inside.

The walk-in vault was a fortified gray room, more wide than

long, with shelves, cabinets, desks, and multiple pushcarts stocked with shrink-wrapped cash. The building was configured so vans could drive inside and pull up next to the vault. That way, outsiders couldn't see money being loaded. In preparation for what lay ahead, David had backed an unmarked company Ford Econoline van near the vault entrance and opened the van's back door.

Moving the money into the van quickly proved an onerous task. Though much of the cash was already stacked on pushcarts in the vault, other stacks were on shelves or the floor, and they were heavy. David was thin—six-foot-one, one hundred sixty-five pounds—and heaving the stacks onto the cart, pushing the cart toward the vault door, and then emptying its contents into the van was exhausting.

And once he started, he didn't stop with one cartful. As beads of sweat formed under his red hair, he loaded up another cart and repeated the process. Seven p.m. came and went, and so did 7:20. Kelly called, using David's own cell phone, to ask where he was already, because she and the others were waiting outside for him.

"I'm busy," he said. "I don't have time to mess with you. I gotta go."

He knew they were nervous outside waiting for him, but he also knew he wouldn't stop stealing until he had taken everything. There was no reason to leave anything, he felt. In the grand scheme of things, the prison sentence for stealing $20 million wouldn't be much worse than for stealing just $500,000—maybe a few extra years behind bars. It wasn't how much you stole that mattered most; it was that you had stolen in the first place.

Each cart, holding about $2 million, was taking David seven or eight minutes to stack, push, and empty into the van, and there were about eight cartloads' worth in the vault. He stayed at it until the vault was empty.

Now, at 7:45 p.m., with all the money finally inside the van, his aching muscles could take a breather. But he wasn't finished. He shut the empty vault and set its timer so the vault could not be opened for two or three days. He also stole both existing sets of vault keys and hurried into the manager's office, where three TV security screens and two VCRs were visible. He realized his bosses would know he had worked that day and that he was missing, but maybe without a video they would think he'd been held at gunpoint and taken hostage, or even better, that he'd been killed. He ejected the two VCR tapes that he knew had recorded him stealing the money, took them, and prepared to leave.

He called Kelly to say he was coming and hopped into the driver's seat of the loaded Loomis van. The plan was to exit through the building's electronic back gate, which consisted of horizontal metal plates that opened at the touch of a button. It should have been easy, but for some reason the gate didn't open for him.

His eyes widened and he stopped breathing as he realized that something as mundane as a malfunctioning gate might ruin their entire plan. He'd already done enough, he realized, to get himself fired and arrested, even if the gate prevented him from moving the money outside the building. He tried again to make the back gate rise, to no avail.

He called Kelly, and a plan B arose—to exit through the

building's front gate instead. This was less desirable than the original plan, because after exiting the front gate he'd still have to deal with a chain-link fence surrounding that part of the building. In addition, if David was going to exit through the front gate, he'd have to move two other Loomis vans parked inside the building that blocked his way. He entered each one, turned the ignition, and drove a few feet so his path was open.

He sighed with relief when the front gate rose, drove the van outside, and hopped out to open the chain-link fence. But nothing was coming easy. Now the chain-link fence was the problem, as he couldn't manage to open it. He pushed. He tugged. Kelly and the others, in two waiting vehicles, watched and shook their heads.

Finally, after minutes that seemed like hours, he received help from an unknown source. A black-haired man popped out of a Mazda 626 and approached the gate, twisting his body around so David wouldn't see his face. David wondered if the man was Steve.

There was no time for introductions. The man helped David swing open the gate. David drove the Loomis van out to the street, and the man hustled back to the Mazda where another, larger man waited. The three-vehicle caravan was ready. Kelly would lead in her pickup truck, David would follow in the Loomis van, and the Mazda would take the rear.

They drove down Suttle Avenue, passing grassy Bryant Park. To the right, between the park's trees, the thieves could've caught a glimpse of Charlotte's skyline of bank buildings in the twilight, about two miles away. It included the sixty-story NationsBank edifice and the slightly smaller First Union Bank building, head-quarters for the two banks that rightfully owned most of the money David was driving into the night.

The Charlotte skyline didn't catch their attention. They headed down Morehead Street to Freedom Drive, a main road that passed industrial buildings, gas stations, and fast-food restaurants toward Interstate 85.

David pulled out a cigarette, put it in his mouth, and maneu-vered his non-driving hand to light it. In the course of just two hours, his life had dramatically changed, and now he couldn't take back what he'd done even if he wanted to. He needed a smoke.

Right about then, he noticed a Charlotte-Mecklenburg Police car in front of him. He shuddered, spitting the unlit cigarette onto the floor. If the cop stopped him, that would be it. David did everything he could to play normal and not draw attention. It worked.

After two miles on Freedom Drive and then five more on Interstate 85 South, the three vehicles exited the highway onto Sam Wilson Road and turned onto a service road for industrial buildings. Those buildings included a printing business called Reynolds & Reynolds, their next destination.

The gate of Reynolds & Reynolds opened for them. On a Saturday night, its emptied parking lot was as good as a private warehouse; no one was around.

Once inside the printing company's gate, the two men exited the Mazda. David got out of the Loomis van, leaving his com-pany handgun and the two security videotapes but taking with him a massive key ring that held about 125 keys. He gave the key ring to the man who had helped him open the chain-link fence, placing the correct key for the Loomis van's back door in the man's hand. Then David hurried to the passenger door of Kelly's pickup truck and hopped inside. She was in the driver's seat, ready to go.

"Let's get out of here," he said.

Teamwork

Kelly drove back to Interstate 85, and David's escape was under way. The plan was for her to drop him off at Columbia Metropolitan Airport in South Carolina, a ninety-minute drive from Charlotte. The group had assumed that security guards at the nearby Charlotte airport—just ten minutes away—would already be looking for David, and that even if he managed to leave from there, the FBI would track down people using the airport that night, show them David's picture, and find out what plane he took.

He was ecstatic. The only life he had ever known was over, and he was about to come into more money than he could ever have imagined. On the drive to Columbia, the magnitude of his actions began to hit him. He held out wads of the stolen cash, gripping green stacks that totaled a year's salary for him.

"I'm richer with what's in my hand right now," he said, "than I've ever been." He changed out of his uniform and laughed with Kelly when she joked, "I'm a *rich* bitch now!"

His exuberance aside, David had an immediate problem, even assuming he could leave the country successfully that night. The vast majority of the millions he'd just stolen were back in the Charlotte area, in a van driven by a man he didn't know, while a woman he loved was driving him south. How would David get his one-third share? The truth is, this actually didn't worry him much.

If that seems strange, it's because he placed a great deal of trust in the notion of teamwork, which he'd say had been drilled into him in the army when he repaired helicopters during the Persian Gulf War. "Gimme a team of five guys and I can do anything," he liked to say. If their plan succeeded, all three of them—David, Kelly, and Steve—would each have more money than they could ever need. For David Ghantt, teamwork was the way to go.

Still, there was the matter of expenses and spending money until his share would arrive in Mexico. David had taken about $50,000 with him, but he wasn't sure how he would sneak it onto a plane past airport security. Kelly had an idea, suggesting they stop at a convenience store to buy pantyhose. A snip here, a snip there, and David had a money belt. He stuffed twenty grand into it, and another five thousand into his cowboy boots. Kelly took the rest.

Back on the road, they soon approached the Columbia airport. It was about 9:30 p.m. now, and Kelly gave David the number for a pay telephone located outside a convenience store just west of Charlotte in a small town called Mount Holly, where she lived. Kelly told him she would wait there for his calls at 1:00 p.m. on Tuesdays and Thursdays.

The Columbia airport seemed quieter than it should have. After Kelly parked, the two of them walked toward the terminal. On the drive down, David hadn't asked about his plane ticket, assuming that Kelly would just pull it out before he left her, or at least that he'd have a reservation waiting for him on a specific flight. After all, if he was sticking his neck out to steal a zillion dollars, the very least his cohorts could do was get him a ticket for that night. But from the moment they pulled into the parking lot, he began worrying the airport was closed for the evening, and it turned out he was right. Once again, the whole plan seemed about to fall apart.

Kelly called Steve from an airport pay phone, and they decided that David's fastest route to Mexico would be through Hartsfield International Airport in Atlanta. But Kelly didn't want to drive the 240 miles to Atlanta and back in the middle of the night, and she didn't know how to find David a bus station, so from a Waffle House pay phone, she called a cab to take him to a bus. A quick kiss, a quick good-bye, and he was gone.

><

As he stared out the window on his bus to Atlanta, David reflected on what had just happened. His life was forever changed, and it was exhilarating. Arriving at the Atlanta airport, he sought a connection to Mexico. He found a flight to New Orleans, where he could then grab an AeroMexico flight to Cancun.

His plane landed in Louisiana before dawn on October 5, and he had time before his connection. Disheveled and sweaty from the previous night's escape and stress, he checked into a hotel in downtown New Orleans, turned the air conditioner on high, and clicked on the television news, expecting to see his face or hear his name. But the theft hadn't made its way to the news yet, probably because it was too early in the morning, he figured. He felt safe enough for the time being and decided to catch a few hours of sleep before his flight to Cancun.

Rested, he took a cab from the hotel to the airport, where another moment of panic awaited. After checking in for his flight, he ordered a slice of pizza at a food court and sat down to eat. Enjoying the calm, he noticed an elderly woman staring at him. He didn't stare back, but her look made him nervous. What was her deal? He pretended not to notice her and began to eat.

She approached him. "Hey, I think I know you!"

He stopped chewing. "Ma'am?"

"Yeah, I know who you are!"

"I don't think so, ma'am."

"You're, you're… Wait a minute."

He couldn't believe it.

"You're that tennis player! The German! Boris Becker!"

Relieved, David exhaled and recited from his fake ID. "I'm Mike," he said. "I'm in computer sales."

The woman left, and David's heartbeat returned to normal. He finished his food and boarded the plane, able to pass unsuspecting police officers with $25,000 around his waist and in his cowboy boots.

At the customs gate after he landed, the officer asked how long David would be in Mexico.

"Two weeks," he answered.

He hopped in a cab outside the airport. David's Spanish consisted mainly of the words "*por favor*" and "*cerveza,*" for "please" and "beer," so he asked the cabdriver in his native tongue to find him a hotel.

"Cheap or 'spensive?" the driver asked.

"'Spensive is okay," David said.

He should treat himself, he figured. The first part of the heist was a success and he was on his way. All he needed was for his coconspirators in North Carolina to follow the plan.

The Key to Success

In his thirty years of life, Steven Eugene Chambers had been a bookie, a tax cheat, and a loan shark, but he had never been into this kind of cash. Few criminals ever had.

For several hours after the theft on October 4, 1997, Steve's well-furnished mobile home near Lincolnton, North Carolina—about forty-five miles from Loomis Fargo—was Heist Central. It was where most of David Ghantt's accomplices counted the money while David fled the country, and it was Kelly's immediate destination after saying good-bye to him in Columbia.

Steve had assumed control of the stolen money shortly after David stole it, from the moment in the Reynolds & Reynolds parking lot when David entered Kelly's pickup and left for the airport. He had waited in his Mazda outside the Loomis Fargo building while David was inside stealing the money, and he was not alone; with him was his cousin Scott Grant, one of two last-minute recruits Steve brought into the plan. Kelly waited nearby, alone in her pickup.

Steve had recruited Scott and another man, Eric Payne, with the promise of $100,000 for each. Scott had said he would help only if there were no guns. Eric, who'd known Steve since they worked at a sock factory as teenagers, insisted he not touch anything. Steve assured them there would be no guns and no need to leave fingerprints. And the job itself would be a piece of cake.

Steve stayed cool during most of the night's excitement and chaos. When David was late coming out of the Loomis building, Scott asked nervously, "What's gonna happen if he don't come?"

Steve calmly answered, "He's coming, he's coming."

Twenty minutes later, when David couldn't open the front gate, Steve directed his cousin to help. When Scott protested, Steve said, "You have to. He can't do it alone." So Scott left the car and hustled to the gate, remembering not to let David see his face.

Steve's Mazda had taken up the rear of the thieves' three-vehicle caravan from Loomis Fargo to Reynolds & Reynolds, where Eric Payne was waiting with a van rented earlier in the day from Budget. As the caravan neared Reynolds & Reynolds, where Eric was an employee, Steve called him so Eric would open the parking-lot gate for them when they arrived.

Steve had caught a glimpse of David before the redhead left with Kelly. Then, along with Eric and Scott, Steve began the next essential task of the heist—transferring the mounds of loot from the Loomis Fargo van to the rented Budget van. The plan then called for abandoning the Loomis vehicle nearby in a secluded area and driving the loaded rental van to Steve's home.

Right away, they had cause for alarm after David left with Kelly. Scott hadn't held onto the exact key that David placed in his hand, and now David was gone and Scott had a key ring filled with about 125 keys, only one of which would open the back of the Loomis van.

In the dark, Scott tried to insert one key after another into the slot. Plenty fit but none would actually turn to open the lock. Steve cursed as Scott continued to fumble with the keys, because the ability to empty the money there and transfer it to the Budget van was an essential piece of the plan. If they couldn't open the back door they might have to abandon the van somewhere with the money inside it, because they certainly couldn't risk being spotted with it the next day after news of the crime broke.

Some frantic minutes later, after dozens of tries, Scott finally found the right key. There was no time to celebrate. He opened the back door.

The vision silenced them. Plastic bags of money in shrink-wrap filled the cargo space almost to the top. Outside of the movies, they had never seen anything like it. Scott's and Eric's jaws dropped.

"Unload it," Steve said.

He directed Eric to hop inside, but Eric refused, not wanting to leave fingerprints. So Steve pushed Scott toward the vehicle. Once inside, Scott began passing stacks of cash to Steve and Eric, who placed them in the rented Budget van, inside fifty-five-gallon blue barrels that Eric had taken from the printing company's loading dock.

As sweat moistened Scott's face and clothes on the cool October evening, he heard a siren in the night. The wailing terrified all three of them as it grew louder. Could the police really have been tipped so soon? Scott walked to the edge of the Loomis van, felt himself stop breathing, put his hands up, and froze.

The siren faded. He saw the flashing lights of an ambulance distancing itself on the highway. Just an ambulance. It seemed like either a cruel joke or a miracle. Relieved, the men got back to work.

Steve's phone rang. It was Kelly, passing an urgent reminder from David to make sure they took the two videotapes that David had left in the Loomis van.

Steve told Scott to grab them, and the men kept working, developing an easy rhythm as the minutes rolled by, taking armloads of cash from the Loomis van, walking a few yards to the Budget van, and filling the plastic barrels with money.

Their haul was so large that the barrels in the rented van couldn't hold it all. They would have to leave millions behind, Steve realized. The alternative—scattering shrink-wrapped cash in the rear of the van—was a nonstarter that would spell doom if a cop pulled them over on the way back to Steve's home, for whatever reason, and made them open the back.

Cool and in charge, Steve told Scott to ignore the stacks of ones and fives and stick to the larger denominations. And leaving money could actually work to their advantage; maybe whoever found it would steal it themselves, drive the van elsewhere, and cloud the group's trail.

The barrels in the rental van were full about forty minutes after the money had arrived at Reynolds & Reynolds. The next task was to abandon the white Loomis van, which of course still had money inside. Scott and Steve handled this while Eric drove the rented van full of loot to a nearby British Petroleum filling station in Mount Holly, where the other two would meet him minutes later.

Scott, followed closely by Steve's Mazda, drove the Loomis van to a wooded area less than a mile from Reynolds & Reynolds, off Moores Chapel Road. Forgetting to turn the car off or take the videotapes, Scott jumped out, closed the door, and hopped into Steve's car.

"Did you cut the van off?"

"No, I kept it running," Scott said.

Steve was not pleased. He had wanted Scott to turn the ignition off. That way, whoever found the van would be able to drive it to a new location that would throw off FBI. But now it was stuck there.

As they approached the BP station to meet Eric at about 9:00 p.m., Scott found yet another reason to worry. A Mount Holly police car was waiting in the gas station's parking lot. "We're gonna get caught," he said worriedly to Steve.

Steve kept his cool. He never flinched in these situations. True, he had never done anything quite like this, but he had a solid career as a small-time crook under his belt. With the officer only dozens of feet from the Budget rental van, Steve left the Mazda and walked nonchalantly to the driver's side of the loaded van while Scott casually slid behind the wheel of the Mazda.

The police officer ignored them.

In two vehicles, the three men left the BP station and drove back onto I-85 and into the heart of Gaston County. "I brought you into this because I trust you," Steve told Eric on the way. "If it went down, I know you wouldn't rat me out." Already, Steve was planning for the worst-case scenario.

As they drove, Steve called Scott on his cell phone to make sure his nervous cousin was all right. Scott said he was fine. The men took Interstate 85 exit to Route 321 North, starting a thirty-minute ride into the northwestern reaches of rural Lincoln County, to Steve's mobile home, which was located near a creek at the end of a gravel road.

There, Steve's wife, Michele, was waiting with ten bags of rubber bands, a calculator, cardboard boxes, and a slashed-and-emptied mattress that one of her children had slept on in a bunk bed before it was gutted.

When the men arrived around 10:00 p.m., the money was finally secured on Steve's property. And it was time to count.

Steve and Eric carried the barrels into the mobile home while Scott looked for something to drink. He knew he had just made the worst mistake of his life and needed to relax, so he grabbed a Sun Drop soda. The twenty-six-year-old plant worker, who had dark hair and a medium build, was clearly out of his element. He had obtained his GED two years earlier and had a six-year-old daughter who lived with her mother, while Scott lived with his girlfriend in a mobile home.

Eric also was nervous. At five-foot-ten and one hundred ninety pounds, with a firm chin and brown mustache, he carried the air of a tough guy. But while he may not have been the nicest guy in the world, he wasn't an experienced criminal. The most serious conviction on his record was for driving while impaired.

The counting began, assembly-line style. Scott passed bundles of cash to Eric, who passed them to Steve, who called out the amounts written on the bundles to Michele, who added everything up on the calculator.

Scott stopped counting when he reached $100,000. "We're gonna get caught," he said. "We're gonna get caught."

Steve told him to calm down. "We won't get caught," he said, "if everyone does what they're supposed to do."

"We're gonna get caught," Scott repeated, staring wide-eyed at the floor.

Michele, keeping tabs, just laughed. "Look at all this money!" she exclaimed. "Look at all this money!"

Steve and Michele loaded twenty-dollar bills, in $10,000 stacks several inches thick, into the slashed mattress. They planned to close it up and put it back on the top bunk above where one of their kids slept.

Scott stopped pacing and leaned against the kitchen counter, folding his hands across his chest and staring at the mattress. "Jesus," he told Michele. "If that falls on your son's head, it's gonna kill him." When the mattress was full of cash, Steve took one end and told Michele to grab the other. They tried to lift it together, but it was too heavy. So they unloaded the cash from it and returned it to the barrels.

Steve, calm throughout, swore everyone in the group to eternal silence.

As Scott got ready to go home, Steve reminded him to stay calm. The count had reached $2.7 million, and Scott just couldn't bear to be around anymore, though his nervousness didn't keep him from carrying $6,000 with him as a first installment. He would have taken more, but he didn't want his girlfriend to suspect anything. While fearing he would be arrested that night, he somehow managed to fall asleep next to her after returning home, only to be awakened by a loud pounding on the door and shouts of "Police! It's the police!" Panicked, he again wondered how everything could have fallen apart so fast. But it turned out to be just a drunken relative.

The others at Heist Central continued counting after Scott left, past midnight. Kelly joined them after her drive from Columbia. The total was more than $14 million. Michele wrote the amount on paper. "I'm rich," she said, laughing again. "I *love* this money!"

Steve placed dog food over the money in the barrels and moved them to a shed behind his mobile home, securing the shed with a Master Lock. He went to sleep at 6:00 a.m.

When he awoke four hours later, he set about the task of moving the money from his home to other locations. He sent Michele to rent space at a storage facility about a mile from their home, and on her return he placed the barrels in the back of their Ford pickup truck. Together they drove to the storage facility to leave the money. Later, Steve would also bury $150,000 in a duffel bag off a trail behind his mobile home.

In the coming days, Steve would better secure the stolen cash. On October 6, Scott's brother, Nathan Grant, and

Nathan's girlfriend, Amy, helped Steve move it to two facilities he felt were more secure, Bubba's Mini Storage and Lincoln Self Storage. Steve had arranged for Nathan, a twenty-year-old mill worker, to rent locker space there, lying to him by saying he was just hiding gambling winnings. Before bringing the money over they stashed it in duffel bags, cardboard boxes, and suitcases. The facilities had gates that allowed vehicles to pass once the driver punched in security codes. Only Steve and Nathan kept the keys to the lockers inside.

For their help, Steve would pay Nathan and Amy $70,000. The small circle of heist beneficiaries was widening.

Creative Money Laundering

Earlier that day, October 6, Michele Chambers, holding a black briefcase filled with cash, had walked into a NationsBank branch office in Mount Holly, about six miles west of the scene of the crime. She had approached the teller, a woman with glasses.

Michele tried to sound self-assured. "How much cash can I deposit," she asked the teller, "without you having to file paperwork?"

The teller told her $10,000, in accordance with a federal law mandating that banks file "suspicious activity reports" when customers make large cash deposits, or when they ask about structuring deposits to avoid filling out forms. The teller didn't say so, but the purpose of the reports was to alert authorities to possible money laundering.

Michele opened her briefcase on the ledge beneath the teller's window, reached into it, and removed bands of twenty-dollar bills totaling $9,500.

The teller kept her eyes steady, saying nothing out of the ordinary. But Michele, sensing the teller thought she was crazy, felt a need to reassure. "Don't worry," she said. "It's not drug money."

The teller accepted the bundles, and Michele left.

Once outside, she hopped into the waiting Mazda 626 with her husband, Steve, who was in the driver's seat. They did not see the teller, inside the bank, fill out a suspicious activity report. The FBI itself wouldn't see the report for about three months, as the paperwork had to go through official channels. But on this day, less than forty-eight hours after the crime, NationsBank, which rightfully owned some of the stolen money, was unwittingly helping the thieves store a portion.

Steve and Michele didn't plan to live much longer in their mobile home, an abode ill-befitting the newly minted millionaires. Steve had told his accomplices not to spend the money wildly, but he and his wife had already made plans to trade up. A few weeks before the heist they had begun searching for a luxury house, even signing with a real-estate agent. Looking at homes priced at $200,000 and higher, they had settled on a 7,000-square-foot beauty with a curved staircase, a stucco exterior, and a price tag of $635,000. It was high on a small mountain in Gaston County, North Carolina, where Steve and Michele had grown up.

On October 5, the day after the theft, Steve and Michele signed an offer to buy it, setting a closing date for later in the month. They agreed to pay $10,000 up front as good-faith money, $400,000 in cash, and $225,000 in financed payments. The Chamberses had been a couple for about five years, and the prospect of moving excited them.

Michele, a former office manager for an insurance company, went by the nickname "Shelley." An attractive woman and a snazzy dresser, she had 34C breasts that were just ten months old and that she wasn't shy to show people, having paid about $4,000 for implants the previous December. They had been a Christmas present to herself, she would say.

Michele had grown up just outside the small town of Mount Holly, and though her parents divorced when she was a kid, she had a relatively normal childhood until she was thirteen years old. That's when she and her mom, Sandra Floyd, fell into a bitter argument over her not coming straight home from cheerleading practice one day. Sandra told Michele she couldn't be a cheerleader. Michele told her mom she was moving out.

She then moved in with her father, but he and Michele had trouble too. At age nineteen, she married a man named Norman Harris, who would join the marines after they had a child together. They later had a second kid. A young mother, Michele had wanted children sooner rather than later because she knew she'd soon need a partial hysterectomy due to a health condition.

Before Norman Harris joined the armed forces and left Michele to fend for herself with a child and a job that couldn't pay the bills, he innocently introduced her to Steve Chambers, who at the time was dating Norman's sister, Angel. Steve and Michele didn't get along, especially when Steve sided with Norman in their arguments.

He was a fast talker, this Steve Chambers. He had a brown goatee and a six-foot-one, two-hundred-twenty-pound build that straddled the line between stocky and fat. He'd held low-paying jobs but had come to see a more promising future in loan-sharking and bookmaking.

Steve's friends knew him to be fascinated by the Northeastern mob culture, at least as he had seen it portrayed by Hollywood in *Goodfellas* and the *Godfather* movies. His lines included "Don't tell nobody nothin'" and "Keep your mouth shut," not to spoof Robert De Niro but as part of his own style. He took his friends to eat at Godfather's Pizza. He flashed phony IDs.

His friends didn't know that Steve had an unusual relationship with the FBI, as an informant for crimes that hadn't actually happened—crimes that he and his friends had only been discussing. He once revealed supposed plans for an armored-car robbery that never materialized. Steve even had a favorite agent, Phil King, who he would call to ask how much money he could receive for information related to specific crimes. Steve didn't know the FBI had written him off as an informant.

From a young age, Steve had associated with people who had criminal histories, and he dropped out of East Gaston High School in the tenth grade. He drove a truck for a while, worked for Coca-Cola, and pulled off some petty crimes with friends.

When Norman Harris asked Steve to look after Michele while he served in the marines, Steve took the request seriously. Too seriously. He spent quality time with Michele and the kids, bringing food to their apartment and helping them get by. He would hug and kiss the kids, read to them, and take them out.

This didn't go unnoticed by their mother, who, one day as Steve was about to leave, told him she loved him. He told her he loved her too, and their lips met.

Michele and her mother had repaired their relationship by then. But Sandra Floyd wasn't pleased with her daughter's infidelity. That's why she and Steve Chambers didn't get along. But there was nothing she could do. Soon enough, Michele and Norman were divorced, and in November 1996, Michele married Steve.

Steve's next bit of heist business was 530 miles away, and since he didn't like flying, he had to take a car. The week after the theft, he and Eric Payne drove to a motel in Evansville, Indiana, to give $50,000 to a man named Mike McKinney. Steve had met McKinney when McKinney was on leave from the marines with Norman Harris, who took him to Gastonia. These days McKinney was working construction. He had given Steve his birth certificate and social security card, which Steve said a friend of his needed to use after fleeing the country due to a shooting. But actually he had passed them to David Ghantt, through Kelly, for his use in Mexico. Now it was time for McKinney's payment.

This wouldn't be the first time Steve had given McKinney money; just after the theft, he had wired him $2,000 to help him pay a fine for driving while intoxicated.

On this day, October 15, 1997, Steve had a suitcase packed with $50,000 in shrink-wrapped ten-dollar bills. He opened it at the motel, took the cash out, and counted it.

Eric asked McKinney, "Do you know where this came from?"

Steve shushed Eric and told McKinney that somebody else had stolen the money from the Mafia. Then he took McKinney aside and offered him a job. "There's a guy who needs to be taken out," Steve said quietly. "Do you want it?" The marines had booted McKinney after his urine tested positive for cocaine, but he still knew how to use a gun. Steve told him he would pay him $250,000 in cash.

McKinney said he would do it, and Steve said he would provide details later. From Steve's perspective, killing David Ghantt would eliminate the heist's top suspect and lessen, if not eliminate, the possibility that the FBI would connect Kelly and him to the heist. And then Steve and Kelly could split David's share between them.

As he traveled, Steve kept in contact with Michele at home. One night, when she mentioned a thunderstorm that was roaring through the county, Steve's thoughts understandably turned to the $150,000 he had buried near their home in a duffel bag. Michele had to retrieve it, he said, or it would turn to mush. But Michele didn't know where it was, and for obvious reasons Steve hadn't marked the site. He gave her directions over the phone.

In the pouring rain, under dark skies illuminated only by lightning, Michele gave it her all. On her knees, in tears, she dug with her hands in the dirt, trying to follow Steve's directions. But her efforts were fruitless, and in twenty minutes it made sense to give up. Steve would have to find the money himself. When he arrived home two days later, he quickly located the duffel bag. Not unexpectedly, the money was soaked and stuck together.

What followed was the only type of money laundering that wouldn't get Steve in trouble. At Steve's behest they placed the green gobs in their laundry dryer and clicked the delicate cycle. Before they turned it on, Steve suggested they throw poker chips in with the "wash," saying he had once heard this could help the bills come apart. They waited nearby as the money flipped around inside. Steve's idea worked. The money was still good.

Caught on Video

David Ghantt probably didn't know it was there.

That was the speculation of three FBI agents and the Loomis Fargo manager. The morning after the heist, they were watching the one security tape that astonishingly had not been swiped. Why else would Ghantt have stolen only two tapes when there had been three? The one that remained had been locked in a cabinet in the manager's office, unlike the others, which were in plain view.

FBI agents Dick Womble, Mark Rozzi, and Rick Schwein sat in the Loomis manager's office staring at a TV screen just before noon on October 5. The manager was furious as he watched the video. Ghantt had almost been fired earlier in the week for briefly leaving money unattended outside the city's Federal Reserve building. Was this his revenge for being yelled at? To make matters worse, the stolen money wasn't marked with known serial numbers. This was a disaster.

The agents, on the other hand, were pleased that Ghantt had left a tape behind. The video quality was mediocre—black-and-white, not terribly clear—but it was good enough. All too often, stricken companies realize after it's too late that they haven't replaced security tapes for a long time and that their videos are worthless. But this one left no doubt that Ghantt was the thief. His lean frame and thinning hair were easily recognizable. A prosecutor using this tape would have an easy time in court.

Womble was excited there was a clear suspect, though the amount of money lost remained uncertain. Loomis workers hadn't yet been able to open the vault because Ghantt had set its timer to stay locked through the weekend, and he had stolen the only sets of keys that existed.

Reviewing the video, Womble and the other agents were amazed by how long Ghantt had worked to finish the job. He had started around 6:45 p.m. and didn't finish for about an hour. Clearly, this was the work of an amateur.

They also were astonished by the amount of labor involved in moving what seemed like more than a ton of cash. Even a stronger man would've struggled with those masses of stacked bills. The agents watched the entire video, some of it in fast-forward mode, looking for a glimpse of any other suspects, but no evidence arose that this wasn't a solo performance.

The FBI had been working the case all day. Loomis officials had called the Charlotte-Mecklenburg Police about 9:30 a.m. on October 5, after its employees couldn't open the vault. The police then called the FBI, because most of the money Loomis

Fargo hauled around belonged to banks, and bank robberies are federal crimes.

Schwein, the on-duty agent that weekend, fielded the police call and immediately notified the bureau's violent crime investigators—known in Charlotte's FBI office as Squad Six. Squad Six, which included Womble and Rozzi, regularly investigated bank thefts. In fact, Charlotte's FBI agents had recently helped recover the money stolen by Philip Noel Johnson, who had hidden most of his $18.8 million Loomis stash in a shed in the mountains of western North Carolina.

While talking to the Loomis warehouse manager, the agents learned that the firm suspected three employees it was unable to contact. But one turned up in church, and another also had been located. The only one still missing was Ghantt, who had worked at the warehouse the previous night with a trainee and nobody else, Loomis officials told the FBI. A twenty-seven-year-old vault supervisor, Ghantt had no criminal record. But his near-firing after the Federal Reserve incident supplied a possible motive.

Actually, the warehouse alarm had gone off the night before, because Ghantt had incorrectly programmed it after stealing the money. But the police had arrived and departed, having checked the building's exterior and noticing nothing askance.

If it was true that more than $10 million had been stolen, as Loomis officials suspected, they were dealing with one of the biggest heists in U.S. history. The FBI needed to learn about David Scott Ghantt, as much as possible and as quickly as possible.

The Federal Bureau of Investigation, founded in 1908, has taken advantage of many of the world's technological advances, but the first part of most investigations still involves person-to-person interviews. Besides providing useful information, a good interview can lead to two or three more, each of which can provide tips or other information.

Agent Womble was tasked with interviewing Ghantt's relatives and quickly learned that Ghantt's wife, sisters, and parents were as shocked as the Loomis officials. The wife, Tammy, was distraught that he was missing and said she knew absolutely nothing about what had happened, and Womble believed her. She refused to believe that David was a calculating thief and was convinced that someone put him up to this.

"This is not my David," she told Womble. Her husband was caring, nice, sweet, gentle, and funny.

The previous evening had begun quite uneventfully for her. She ate dinner with her mom at the Cracker Barrel restaurant in Gastonia and called David at work, telling him not to grab anything on the way home. She had takeout for him—chicken and potatoes.

"Refrigerate it," David had told her. "I'll be home late tonight."

"Late" meant around 9:00 p.m., Tammy figured. So she worried when, after awaking at 1:00 a.m., she found herself alone under the covers. She called David at work, then on his pager, then on his cell phone, and then on his pager again. Nothing. She'd always been nervous he might catch a bullet working for Loomis Fargo, with all that money around, and now she was ready to believe the worst.

Finally, at 2:30 a.m., she telephoned David's parents in Hendersonville, nearly two hours west in the North Carolina mountains. They said they'd rush over, and as they made their way to the Ghantts' mobile home in Kings Mountain, Tammy called the authorities. An officer for the Charlotte-Mecklenburg County Police told her they couldn't do anything because David lived in Kings Mountain, which was located in Cleveland County. Then someone at the Cleveland County Sheriff's Office told her *they* couldn't help because David was last seen in Charlotte. Finally, Tammy found a Charlotte-Mecklenburg police officer who promised to start investigating. After she hung up, she paced the floor and stared at framed pictures of David on the wall.

David's parents arrived about 5:00 a.m., exhausted and extremely worried. First thing in the morning, the three of them decided, they would post missing-person fliers of David in Gastonia and Charlotte. Maybe they would look for a private eye, since the cops hadn't seemed very helpful.

In the morning, the authorities called to say they had found David's pickup truck in the Loomis parking lot. Tammy didn't know what to make of that. A few hours later, Mark Rozzi called to ask if she could come to Charlotte's FBI office to talk.

But Tammy had more questions for the FBI than answers. Where was he? Was he even alive? She was desperate for information, but Rozzi had little to offer.

≥≤

At 4:00 p.m., agents John Wydra and Julia Mueller were dispatched to the Loomis warehouse to help other FBI agents with crime-scene work. They examined the building's interior, dusted for fingerprints, and searched Ghantt's abandoned pickup truck. Then they began interviewing current and former Loomis Fargo employees, trying to learn anything they could about Ghantt and the heist.

It came out that Ghantt had few close friends at Loomis. No one at work seemed to know him very well. Wydra and Mueller talked to about twenty Loomis workers, gaining a few tidbits here and there but nothing that revealed a path to his whereabouts. The agents weren't accusatory, but they watched for signals that the employees might be lying. While they learned little of value, they took down names and numbers of a few other people who might know more.

Wydra usually worked for the Charlotte FBI branch's Squad Four, focusing on white-collar crime. His specialty was tracing money laundering. But on this day, almost all the agents were working together with Squad Six, the violent crime unit, trying to sort out what happened and answer basic questions. Was Ghantt dead? If he was alive, where did he go? Did he take all the money with him? Did he leave any clues? And how did he pull this off, anyway?

Early that evening, agents and supervisors assembled at the FBI's headquarters for North Carolina at 400 South Tryon Street in downtown Charlotte. It was becoming apparent that nearly all of Charlotte's FBI agents would be asked to work this case almost exclusively for several days, maybe weeks.

On the ninth floor, around the Squad Six desks and cubicles, Womble and Rozzi briefed the others on what they had learned about Ghantt from his relatives. The sheer boldness of the act had amazed them all. Ghantt seemed to have just taken the money and run, leaving his family behind to wonder. The agents also learned that even now, Loomis Fargo was unable to open the vault to count its losses. The company planned to break into the vault the next day. Meanwhile, Loomis officials were developing a sense of how much was missing—about $15 million, they thought, but they were uncertain. There was only one solid piece of information, compliments of the videotape.

Yet while Ghantt was the only person caught on video, the agents didn't assume he'd worked alone. Some even wondered if an accomplice had shot him afterward. Federal prosecutors, on the other hand, assumed he was still alive. On the afternoon of October 6, an assistant U.S. attorney named David Keesler had Womble read evidence against Ghantt to a federal grand jury that happened to have its regularly scheduled monthly meeting in Charlotte that day.

It was an open-and-shut indictment. By day's end, David Ghantt was charged with bank larceny. For that, the maximum penalty was ten years in prison and a fine. All the agents had to do now was find him.

At about 5:40 p.m. on October 6, soon after Womble completed his testimony to the grand jury, the FBI received a phone call from a man who had just finished mowing his lawn in western Mecklenburg County. He had noticed a seemingly abandoned white vehicle in the woods and said it fit the description of the missing Loomis van broadcast on the news.

Speculation was rampant within the bureau. Maybe all the missing money was inside. Maybe David was there, handcuffed and waiting for them. Maybe all they'd find in the cargo area was his lifeless body.

About six agents and Loomis officials arrived at the wooded area, a lovers' lane littered with beer cans and cigarette butts, late in the afternoon. Immediately, they saw it was the right truck. The doors were locked, so they looked through the tinted windows. Inside, they saw mounds of money, still shrink-wrapped, behind the driver's seat. It was clear to the Loomis officials that most of the stolen money was not there. It was unclear if there was a body inside.

A flatbed truck was called to haul the van to an FBI garage at headquarters, where they could examine its contents in a secure area. There, with FBI supervisor Vic O'Korn present, they opened the vehicle and quickly saw that the stacks of bills inside were mostly ones and fives. The thieves had taken the larger denominations. On the front seat were David Ghantt's gun and the two other Loomis surveillance videotapes that had been stolen. No one knew why he had left them behind.

Counting the money took only half an hour, as the wrappers around the stacks were marked with their totals: $3.3 million altogether, less than one-fifth of the stolen amount. The FBI knew this because Loomis had used heavy machinery to break through the vault's steel-and-concrete wall earlier in the day and determined the total take: $17,044,033.

Mileage records for the van showed it hadn't been driven far after the heist. But the value of that information seemed minimal, given that most of the money had obviously been off-loaded. Perhaps David had rented another vehicle nearby. FBI supervisors dispatched agents to show Ghantt's picture at rental-car companies in town, but none of the clerks recognized his face. The agents were awash in dead ends.

Yet the more the FBI learned about the basic circumstances of the case, including the abandonment of the truck, the more likely it seemed that David Ghantt had accomplices. Pulling this off alone would've been too difficult. A solo act would've required him to have planted the rental van in the secluded area where the Loomis vehicle was eventually found, and then, after the theft, to have transferred the money from the Loomis van into that rental vehicle.

There were problems with this scenario. First, presumably Ghantt would've needed a ride from someone after planting the rental van in the woods. Second, the weight and volume of the money stolen—more than a ton, at 2,748 pounds and sixty-four cubic feet of bills—seemed too large for such a skinny man to have moved twice in the same evening. That he had accomplished it even once, from the vault to the Loomis van, seemed remarkable enough.

Then there was the question of the money left behind. If Ghantt had acted alone, the thinking went, he probably would have made proper accommodations for all the money he stole. Perhaps, according to this theory, he had accomplices whose vehicle was just too small to fit everything. In either case, the FBI noted the thief's or thieves' presence of mind in focusing on the large bills. The $3.3 million in recovered cash was almost entirely in smaller bills. While it constituted only one-fifth of the total amount stolen, it comprised two-fifths of the weight.

><

An important tip emerged the week after the theft, after agents Wydra and Mueller interviewed more past and current Loomis employees. A few said that Ghantt had recently mentioned he was dating a former worker there, a woman named Kelly Jane Campbell. The interviewees said she was full of attitude, the kind of person who blurted out whatever came to mind. She had stopped working at Loomis about a year earlier.

The dominant early impression the agents had of Ghantt was that of a loner, so if his colleagues were mentioning a girlfriend, she was worth talking to. They decided to check her out. Wydra and Mueller continued interviewing Loomis employees while two other agents drove to Kelly Campbell's home on Tuesday.

The route took agents Gerry Senatore and David Martinez from the well-tailored streets of Charlotte's banking district to the back roads of rural Gaston County. Approaching their destination, the agents turned off a two-lane road onto a gravel street that looked like it dead-ended into tall trees but actually continued into hidden, winding asphalt roads that passed a compound of mobile homes unseen from the main street. At the end of the road, Kelly Campbell lived in a white mobile home surrounded by the goats, dogs, and roosters kept by her and her husband, Jimmy, nicknamed "Spanky."

The agents knocked on her door. She opened it.

Tall and pleasantly plump with dirty-blond shoulder-length hair, Kelly Campbell didn't smile often, even around people she could tolerate. When she did smile, it was worth it. Her eyes sparkled and the grin she displayed was sweet.

But she wasn't smiling now. She begrudgingly let the FBI agents inside and called her father to babysit her daughter for a while. Seated in her living room, the agents told her that people at Loomis Fargo said she and David Ghantt had dated. Could she tell them anything about where he was?

Campbell said she'd heard about the heist but didn't know anything about it. She and Ghantt were friends, she said, but that was it. They hadn't dated. She described him as quick tempered and goofy and said they had smoked some pot together, but that was it.

The agents didn't care about her pot smoking, but they wanted to see if she was telling the truth. They asked if she had any marijuana at home. She said she did. One agent asked her to bring it out to them.

"Why?" she asked. "So you and your buddy can go down the road and smoke it?"

She brought out about an ounce. The other Loomis employees were right about her, the agents thought; Kelly Campbell spoke her mind.

When they changed the subject, asking if she had any idea where Ghantt was, Kelly offered that he liked the mountains and maybe was staying around Hendersonville or Wilkesboro, North Carolina, where his parents lived.

The agents then asked if she would take a lie-detector test.

She declined. They were persistent, but they couldn't sway her. Investigators often view reluctance to take a lie-detector test as a sign a suspect is hiding something, but in this case, the agents realized, what she might have been hiding was drug use or a possible affair with David. It certainly didn't seem from her surroundings that she had come into money recently.

They left but decided they would keep an eye on her.

How Baseball Hindered the FBI

"Van, Driver, Money Missing," shouted the lead headline on the front page of the *Charlotte Observer*, the biggest newspaper in the Carolinas, on October 6, 1997. "A very substantial amount of money," possibly as much as $15 million, had vanished, along with an armored car and the driver, David Ghantt, the story said. It continued, "If the money was stolen and that amount is correct, this would be one of the largest heists in U.S. history. The same company, Loomis, Fargo & Co., lost $18.83 million in March in a heist in Jacksonville, Florida."

Ghantt was six-foot-one and had strawberry blond hair and blue eyes, according to the newspaper and the TV news on Monday. He weighed about one hundred sixty-five pounds and had a tattoo of a pistol and a rose on his left arm, the FBI said.

Over the next twelve months, the heist would rank high among the biggest news stories in the Carolinas, and the media already planned to monitor the investigation closely. In the days afterward, *Observer* editors dispatched two reporters to Ghantt's mobile home to gather information about him from his relatives. But the man answering the door politely asked them to leave.

Tammy and David's other relatives were too upset to talk with the press. So most of what was printed was basic biographical material from the FBI and public records. Reporters suspected that if David was alive, he was far away, though some suggested that anybody who would steal that much cash might be dumb enough to stay near the scene of the crime.

Gary German hoped David Ghantt was nearby, just because the story would be funnier that way. German was not a reporter looking for a big scoop; rather, he was one of the strangest steady newspaper sources the *Observer* ever had. A talkative, foul-mouthed man permanently bedridden from a car accident and fascinated by local crime, he did little with his time but listen to police scanners to hear officers' radio transmissions of interesting breaking news.

He then took it upon himself to alert newspapers and TV stations to nighttime street trouble that had slipped beneath their radar. The local media gladly accepted the help. Since they often lacked the money to fully staff their newsrooms twenty-four hours a day, night-owl Gary's early-morning calls to TV camera crews helped them reach crime scenes before the bodies were taken away. Such footage virtually ensured that a story made the TV news.

Indeed, Gary lived off Gaston County crime, getting monthly checks from newspapers and TV stations for his calls. He claimed that he gave booze to select local law-enforcement officers in exchange for news tips, and he called reporters at home in the middle of the night when he deemed the events of the streets newsworthy. During the day, he would phone the newspapers' crime reporters in Gaston County and tell them about the most recent incidents, not even bothering to say hello but starting out with the likes of, "Got yourself a shootin' on Airline Avenue. That sumbitch emptied his bullets and got his ass *outta* there."

Gary's law-enforcement friends did not include FBI agents, so he had nothing of value to share with the media on the heist. The FBI was not telling the press about Kelly Campbell, revealing only that David Ghantt might have had help.

The first week after the heist, FBI agents worked sixteen-hour days. Womble stayed in touch with Tammy Ghantt and David's other relatives, trying to reconstruct David's forty-eight hours prior to the theft to determine motives that might reveal where he'd gone. But the FBI agent learned little of value except that David was an avid reader of detective novels. All that meant for the FBI was that David might have considered their investigative techniques and had probably been thinking about the crime for a while.

Womble, Rozzi, and other agents posted fliers of Ghantt in the area, hoping someone would spot him and call the authorities. On their own, people were calling the FBI with supposed sightings of Ghantt at the airport or at a topless bar—leads that wound up going nowhere. Agents also drove to hotels to check registration books and show Ghantt's picture to clerks in case he had used a phony name to check in. John Wydra and other agents interviewed workers at businesses near the Loomis Fargo building on Wilkinson Boulevard to see if anybody had heard or seen anything unusual the night of the theft. The only clue came from the manager at a sandwich shop call Niko's Grill, who said Ghantt had eaten lunch there hours before the theft. Of course, this information went nowhere.

A significant indication that Ghantt had help popped up a week after the theft, through information presented in twice-daily FBI briefings for the agents on the case. The clue came from numbers entered into Ghantt's pager from right before and during the theft. Most of the calls were from his own mobile-phone number. He hadn't called it himself, it seemed safe to assume. Someone else had to be using his phone, a clever attempt to keep the accomplice in the clear.

But one number sequence repeated often in the pager seemed intriguing: 143, 143, 143. At first, the agents—most of them in their thirties and forties—had no idea what it meant. But one of them soon realized that he'd read about the code in a recent newspaper article about beeper-speak. It meant "I love you." Another agent, Phil King, recalled that his daughter's boyfriend often punched 143 into her pager.

The FBI didn't know who had entered the code, but the numbers were a sign that a woman besides his wife probably had communicated with Ghantt during the theft. Whether that woman was Kelly Campbell or not was unclear, but at the very least Ghantt seemed to have someone on the side who probably knew what he had done.

The clock was ticking. The first week of the investigation was mostly a bust, and the forty agents all knew that solving a case like this grows more difficult as time passes. Evidence disappears. Potential witnesses leave town, forget information, or even die. The criminals themselves can move farther and farther away.

The FBI hoped the TV show *America's Most Wanted* could help. On October 11, most of the agents gathered at headquarters to watch a segment of the show featuring Ghantt that was scheduled to air across the country. The start time on the East Coast was 9:00 p.m. Other agents positioned themselves on the city's streets so they could quickly check the flood of tips expected to barrage the bureau after the show. Meanwhile, these agents canvassed every business located on the most direct route from the Loomis Fargo warehouse to where the van was found in the woods. They asked if anyone had seen anything suspicious on October 4. Nobody had.

The bulk of the staff waited at headquarters for the show to begin. First broadcast in 1988, *America's Most Wanted* has been credited with helping to catch more than 1,200 criminals. Wydra, Rozzi, supervisor Rick Shaffer, and others watched baseball on the TV in the command post, a playoff game between the Cleveland Indians and Baltimore Orioles. *America's Most Wanted* would be on the same channel right after the game.

At first, the room filled with anticipation over potential new tips. But the baseball score soon became a concern. It was tied late in the game, and the prospect of extra innings loomed as 9:00 p.m. approached. If neither team scored, the game threatened to prevent the Ghantt segment of the show from airing. Maybe, the agents hoped, the network would air all of the show anyway after the game. They didn't know how that would work.

To the dismay of everyone present, the game didn't end until almost 10:00 p.m., when the Indians' Marquis Grissom crossed home plate in the twelfth inning, four hours and fifty-one minutes after the game began. It was the longest League Championship Series game in baseball history.

The agents saw that the station would still air the show after the game, but not the whole episode. When it came on, details of another crime were being shown, and then quickly a commercial filled the screen. Maybe the Ghantt segment would run next, they hoped.

When the show returned after commercials, the agents heard the narrator telling viewers to call in if they saw David Ghantt. Clearly, the Ghantt segment was over, without anyone on the East Coast having seen it. The agents cursed and fired wadded paper and crumpled Doritos bags at the screen. Supervisor Shaffer, an Indians fan, held his head in his hands. Wydra and the others were furious. Only western viewers would see it that night.

The agents positioned on the street learned nothing valuable. The FBI would receive one Ghantt tip that evening, from someone who thought he had seen Ghantt gambling in Las Vegas. The caller didn't even know the name of the casino.

⊰⊱

The FBI believed David Ghantt's wife, Tammy, when she said the day after the crime that she knew nothing about the heist. And surveillance of her had turned up nothing. She even helped in the taping of the *America's Most Wanted* segment, ending it by pleading to her husband, "Please, if there's any way possible, call us or the FBI and let us know you are alive and well… And remember, David, no matter what, we do love you."

Agents gave her a lie-detector test anyway, on October 11, just to be on the safe side. Though the results of lie-detector tests are not considered reliable enough to be allowed as evidence at trials, many agents, detectives, and prosecutors find them useful tools for investigations.

Agent Bob Drdak conducted the test, asking Tammy some basic questions.

Had she seen David since the theft?

She said she hadn't.

Had she talked to him since?

Again, she said she hadn't.

Strangely, the test results came back inconclusive. This surprised the agents, who assumed she would easily pass. They decided to test her again two days later, on October 13. Drdak started by asking Tammy if she wanted to change any of her answers from the first test.

What she said probably explained why she hadn't passed the first time. She explained to Drdak that the other day, when he'd asked if she'd seen David, she'd thought of her husband's picture near the foot of her bed. She had seen the picture, as well as their home videos, which was like seeing him, she had thought. So maybe she hadn't answered that question with certainty. The same was true when he asked if she'd talked to David. Since the theft, she had called his voice mail and heard his voice.

Drdak explained that he was interested only in whether she had actually seen him alive or heard him speak to her live. He then rephrased his polygraph questions accordingly.

"Besides seeing his picture in your bedroom or on home videos, have you seen David since the theft?"

"No," Tammy said.

"Besides on voice mail, have you heard his voice since the theft?"

"No," she said.

Tammy passed. And while their belief in her credibility did nothing to help them find David, it helped them to feel sure that she wasn't lying.

Nerves

Kelly Campbell was nervous and scared. And when Kelly Campbell was nervous and scared, she smoked pot. Lots of it.

In the two weeks after the heist, Kelly, twenty-seven, was smoking marijuana morning, noon, and night. And she had solid reasons to be nervous and scared. After all, she had lied point-blank to the FBI when the agents came to her door. She had indeed been in contact with David, having received a page when he arrived in Mexico. She knew she couldn't pass a lie-detector test and dreaded the prospect of agents returning to pressure her.

After the agents left her, she had called Steve Chambers for advice. He told her not to worry about it, that he had a lawyer who would call the FBI on her behalf. The lawyer would help keep her out of trouble and say she wasn't going to take the test.

Steve had told Kelly the Loomis money was hidden "up north" with three men he knew who ran a crooked bank that was charging them a fee. And the reason he had a lawyer was because the local police had recently arrested Steve in an unrelated case, from before the heist, for writing $30,000 in fraudulent checks. His lawyer, a short, salt-and-pepper-haired man named Jeff Guller, was negotiating a plea bargain for Steve that could keep him out of jail. Steve would have to plead guilty to forty-two counts of obtaining property by false pretenses, a felony.

Guller met with Kelly, who told him she didn't want to take a lie-detector test. He didn't press her on it. He took the business card the agents had given her, called the FBI, and left a voice-mail message saying he represented Kelly Campbell and that she didn't want to take a polygraph. Kelly didn't know how useful this would be, but at least she now had professional help.

That Kelly and Steve had been in touch at all the previous year was because of a much smaller scam than the one linking them now. They had grown up together, their friendship formed at teenage drinking parties off the back roads of Gaston County, but they had lost touch after high school. Then, sometime in the mid-1990s, Steve contacted Kelly with a scam in mind. He wanted to pay her for her husband's employee number on his W-2 tax form, which Steve would use to file a phony tax return. She obliged.

She and Steve began hanging out. In late 1996, after having recently quit her job at Loomis Fargo, Kelly found herself in Steve's yard, listening to music with a bunch of his friends, grilling steaks, drinking, and playing Uno. At one point, Steve verbally cornered her about the ins and outs of her experience working at Loomis Fargo. *How many people work on an armored truck? When is the best time of day to knock one off? Was there anyone there who might team up with them?*

And so it was that momentum for a heist of historic proportion originated over Budweiser and a game of Uno outside a mobile home in rural North Carolina. Steve had pondered a heist of his own for years—it seemed doable, he thought. But on that day, Kelly shot him down.

"Don't even think about it, Steve," she said. "It's too dangerous. Armored-car drivers carry guns."

Steve persisted. Maybe, he suggested, they could plant phony hand grenades on the armored truck and steal the money when the guards ran away. He'd heard of that approach used elsewhere.

"Yeah, okay, Steve," Kelly told him, rolling her eyes.

But when she left that day, the idea stayed with her. Her life felt in need of change, dramatic change. She and her husband, Jimmy, had recently declared bankruptcy, and despite a promotion at her security-guard job, she couldn't envision dramatically improving her lot. Plus, her marriage was failing.

All she wanted was a house in the country, a swimming pool for her two kids, and a divorce. So she kept thinking about making Steve's idea a reality and about asking David if he would do it. She had faith that Steve could help them succeed. After all, he was always talking about his mysterious activities "up north," and he seemed to have lots of money for someone without a full-time job.

In the following months, Steve repeated the idea to Kelly a few more times. Still, until the middle of summer, it remained just a silly thing between the two of them. Then, on a late afternoon in August 1997, Kelly decided to page David at work and see if she could put the plan into motion.

Steve had told Kelly to lie to David if that was needed to persuade him, and that's what she did. She didn't love David. She didn't want to move to Mexico. She didn't want her kids to grow up on the run in a different country. But she wanted David to steal the money so she could become rich. So, in the back of her pickup truck two weeks before the heist, she let him kiss her. He was thrilled.

The idea was to keep the inner circle small, but in the days before the heist Steve told her that he had recruited two others, Eric Payne and Scott Grant, to help. Kelly didn't object. "You're the one with all the brains, Steve," she told him. "You know what you're doing."

On the afternoon of October 4, the day of the theft, the group—minus David—met at the parking lot of a discount store in Belmont, North Carolina, just west of Charlotte. Then, when David told Kelly on the phone that he wouldn't be ready until 7:00 p.m. at the earliest, they crossed the street to a bowling alley to pass the time. While Kelly ate a cheeseburger and fries, Eric Payne sidled up to her and asked, "Is this really gonna happen?"

"Yeah," Kelly said. "I don't believe it, but yeah, it's gonna happen."

Fun on the Run

By mid-October, two weeks into his new life, the skinny redhead was not quite as skinny as he'd been before.

While the FBI checked up on Kelly back home, and while David's picture was featured prominently in American newspapers, he was living the life of a rich international fugitive, enjoying the white-sand beaches of Cancun while trying to keep a low profile among the tourists.

He didn't know exactly how much he'd stolen from Loomis Fargo, having not counted the stacks as he grabbed them, but he estimated it was between $14 million and $15 million. He eagerly awaited his one-third share. For the time being, the $25,000 he took with him the night of the crime was sufficient. He was skipping from hotel to hotel in Cancun and eating at least four meals a day. He tried lobster for the first time in his life, and then ate it again and again.

Overall, his new wealth was not quick to affect his tastes. His first two meals as a multimillion-dollar thief had been pizza at the airport in New Orleans and a Big Mac Combo at a Cancun McDonald's. His looks changed though. To disguise himself, he'd dyed his hair brown, begun using tanning spray, and had both ears pierced.

Free and rich in Cancun, David often thought back to his last morning in his mobile home a thousand miles north. He remembered waking up at 5:00 a.m. that day, showering, putting on his gray Loomis Fargo uniform, and preparing a pot of coffee. He'd then kissed his sleeping wife on the cheek and taken the garbage out before closing the door on his family life.

He had been careful not to deviate from his normal routine that week, going so far as to schedule a regular dental appointment. Then, on the fateful morning, he packed three days' worth of clothes and a .45-caliber handgun and hopped into his 1996 Dodge Dakota pickup truck. On the way to work, he pulled into a service station and picked up a box of Marlboro Light 100s, a package of crackers, and a Cheerwine, the sweet, cherry-flavored soda of the South.

Then he took Interstate 85 heading east into Charlotte, his normal forty-five-minute commute. As usual, he flipped the radio to his favorite station, which aired the *John Boy & Billy Big Show*, a morning program. As he drove in, the station actually played the Steve Miller Band's "Take the Money and Run."

⋺⋵

His choice of Cancun seemed to validate itself early. After his plane landed on October 5, his taxi drove him down Kukulkan

Boulevard, the main tourist strip. As the beaches and turquoise sea came into view, David realized why Cancun was the perfect place to wait out his heist share.

The cabdriver stopped at the Omni Hotel, a twelve-story flamingo-pink structure. At about $130 a night, it wasn't the most expensive hotel in town, but it would be more than sufficient. Views from the room included sparkling pools, a swim-up bar, the beach, and the Caribbean Sea.

David was mentally drained when he checked in and slept for the better part of the next two days. Then, as his nerves began to ease, he threw himself into Cancun's tourist scene, starting with a shopping spree. The long-sleeve shirts and pants he'd brought from home were meant for October in North Carolina, not Mexico, so he purchased a new wardrobe, laying down cash for silk shirts, four pairs of python-skin cowboy boots, and three pairs of Ray-Ban sunglasses at $200 a pop. He reveled in the nightlife, finding a favorite bar called Christine, which had a huge dance floor.

He ventured beyond the hotel zone. A third-row ticket to a bullfight was a success, giving the once-poor Gaston County boy the chance to yell "*Toro! Toro!*" with the crowd, though a beef-and-cheese snack from a vendor later gave him Montezuma's revenge that knocked him out for three days. Soon afterward, his inner amateur historian led him to tour the famous Mayan ruins at Chichen Itza, located about a hundred miles from Cancun on the Yucatan Peninsula. The attractions included El Castillo, a pyramid built 1,200 years earlier and shaped to represent the Mayan calendar, with eighteen terraces representing its eighteen twenty-day months. He also enjoyed a ball court called Juego de Pelota Principal, which was surrounded by temples where losing captains had been sacrificed in ancient days.

He didn't expect to stay in Cancun for long. There were too many Americans, and he didn't want to be recognized. He planned to seek citizenship elsewhere, maybe Brazil. Wherever he eventually landed, he would buy a fifty-five-foot boat and spend his days on the water. In his spare time, he would follow the heist investigation however he could. And he would find a way to send postcards to his relatives that wouldn't reveal where he was.

In the latter half of October, he spent his days horseback riding, driving Jet Skis, and deep-sea fishing. He soared in an ultralight plane, which made him feel like a bird. He parasailed over the Caribbean, rising higher than the highest Cancun hotel, high enough that he could have shouted a full confession and nobody would have been the wiser. His view from above included the entire Cancun strip and the endless blue sea. With $5 million or so coming his way, he could not have felt happier.

Most days, he woke up around 10:30 a.m., downed a big breakfast, sat on the beach a bit, and only then deigned to consider how he would pass the remainder of the day. He ate wherever he pleased, paying in cash. He had a favorite restaurant, Zandunga, a Caribbean-Mexican grill that served spinach quesadillas, shrimp mounted on a coconut, and flan. Mariachi bands performed while his eyes reveled in the grandeur of the evening sky over the sea.

He ate at Zandunga almost every other day, and the waiters came to know him by the name on his phony ID, Mike McKinney. They called him Mr. Mike and brought him bottles of Dos Equis. He befriended a waiter named Aldo, who spoke some English and helped him find an apartment on the beach. Whenever he met Americans, David generally let them introduce themselves first and then lied about where he was from.

He believed the money coming his way would set him up comfortably for the rest of his life. And this would be wired or smuggled to him shortly, he assumed. Of course, Kelly would eventually be coming to live with him, and they would spend the rest of their lives together, going through money like lunatics and doing whatever they pleased, whether drinking all day, sailing, or just chilling out on the beach. It would be paradise. Kelly was the only person in North Carolina he had spoken with after the heist. He called her every Tuesday.

Their actual relationship was more complicated than the one he had imagined. He told her he loved her and couldn't wait for her to come down; that kiss in the pickup truck had whetted his appetite for more. But she told him she couldn't get away from North Carolina just yet. The FBI had questioned her, she told him, and she was worried they thought she was involved and might be tracking her every move.

David himself, while thoroughly excited by his new life, was increasingly certain he could never return to the United States. He wasn't sure what his future identity would be—maybe Mike McKinney or some character name from a novel by Tom Clancy, his favorite author—but it wouldn't be David Ghantt. David Ghantt probably could never again get a driver's license, buy a house, install a phone, subscribe to a magazine, or use a credit card without David Ghantt getting caught.

He felt no guilt or obligation toward Loomis Fargo and never questioned his decision to clean out the vault. As for Tammy, well, he figured that she would move on. Their marriage had been on the rocks anyway. He worked too many hours, and they hadn't been seeing much of each other. When they did spend time together, they didn't communicate well.

But David's acts of thievery and desertion had devastated his wife, who had done nothing to deserve this treatment and who didn't know why he had left, or even that he hadn't been forced at gunpoint. It was all a mystery to her, and she was struggling emotionally and financially. Her data-entry job couldn't pay the bills, so she tried to refinance the loan on their pickup truck to reduce the monthly payments. But David's name appeared on the title alongside hers, and the Division of Motor Vehicles told her she couldn't remove his name without a court order.

She hired a lawyer, who drew up the appropriate document: "That David Scott Ghantt has been accused and indicted in an alleged incident which took place on October 4, 1997 in Mecklenburg County, North Carolina, in which a large amount of cash was taken from his...employer. That David Scott Ghantt has not been seen nor heard from since the time of the alleged incident and that he may be deceased."

A judge granted the order, and Tammy refinanced their loan. But the bills still were too high, and the truck was soon repossessed. She also struggled to meet their mortgage payments on the mobile home, knowing that if worst came to worst, she could move in with her parents in Gastonia. Indeed, through it all, her family kept her company. David's mother drove down from

Hendersonville to stay with her during the week. On weekends, Tammy stayed at her parents' house, twenty minutes away.

Still, it was emotional torture for her. Each night she wondered if David was dead, and if authorities had checked the Catawba River near where the Loomis van had been found. Maybe he was being held hostage somewhere by someone who stayed out of the camera shot while David moved the money. Why else wouldn't he have called her?

Of course, the possibility that he was alive and well didn't offer her much comfort either. Through it all, Tammy prayed. She prayed for David's safety, that he would come back so they could resume their lives. She prayed with David's mother, a religious woman, and she prayed by herself wherever she was. All she wanted was for him to be home.

She wanted to fix him breakfast and clean for him. Their mobile home had never been so tidy as since he left because she was cleaning it so much. She remembered how they first met, as teenage coworkers at the Winn-Dixie supermarket in Gastonia. She had been working the cash register one day and needed somebody to bag groceries. An eager redhead had approached.

"David Ghantt at your service, ma'am."

"You came to my rescue," she told him.

He liked that she thought of him as her rescuer. They began dating. He would wait outside the store for her shift to end and drive her home. After three months, she ended it. It was just one of those things, she told him. She dated other men, though she often thought back to David.

They rekindled their romance through letters while David was in the army overseas, and he proposed over the phone. He made it official after he was discharged, giving her a diamond ring, then getting on his knees and closing his eyes to ask if she would marry him.

They married on June 20, 1992, at Lakeview Church in the small town of McAdenville. The wedding albums had happy, funny pictures of that day, one of David with two letters taped to each shoe—*PL* on his right sole and *EH* on his left. His sisters had put them there as a joke, hoping his shoes would spell out HELP when he knelt during the service, but they had misplaced the letters. In another wedding picture, David was pretending to escape through a church window. That one wasn't funny anymore.

After their wedding, the Ghantts lived in several places—in Hilton Head, South Carolina; Gastonia; and Kings Mountain. Tammy was content with her life, especially after they bought the mobile home in Kings Mountain. She would come home and see David asleep on the couch, with their cat, Rascals, snuggled on his chest.

They would go on picnics in the area, take weekend drives into the mountains ninety minutes away, and visit David's parents in Hendersonville. They talked about having children in a few years, when Tammy turned thirty. They dreamed that she would open a tanning salon, he would open a hunting ground, and they would have a financially stable family.

Meanwhile, David's mind surged with excitement over the growing legend of David Ghantt, master thief. People would talk about him for years, even decades, he fantasized. And when they did, it would be with admiration, with envy, with intrigue. He would be thought of with the great ones, men like D. B. Cooper, Albert Spaggiari, and Willie Sutton. They would be notable company.

David lacked the daring of Cooper, who on November 24, 1971, had jumped out of a Boeing 727 jet with $200,000 that wasn't his, somewhere between Portland, Oregon, and Seattle, Washington. Earlier that day, with the plane bound for Seattle, Cooper had threatened to blow it up unless authorities arranged to secure him the cash in twenty-dollar bills and parachutes upon landing. He got what he wanted, and after Cooper let the thirty-five passengers go free, he had the plane take off again, directing the pilot to fly toward Mexico City. He jumped out somewhere over the Pacific Northwest, using a rear door.

The crew members didn't know exactly where he jumped because they were in the cockpit, unable to see the back of the plane. Less than $6,000 of the marked bills given to Cooper ever showed up—$5,880 was found in Washington State. Many suspected Cooper died either on impact or soon thereafter. Still, his daring act would inspire decades of admiration most recently reflected in the annual D. B. Cooper Day event that draws hundreds to the Ariel Store and Tavern in Washington State, around where he is thought to have landed. Cooper was a legend.

The same was true of Albert Spaggiari, who in July 1976 stole more than $8 million in money and valuables from the Société Générale bank in Nice, France. On a bulletin board facing the door of the main vault, his gang wrote, "*Sans armes, sans haine, et sans violence*"—"Without weapons, without hatred, and without violence," showing concern for their reputation.

Spaggiari's notoriety stemmed from both his detailed planning—for several weeks, at night, his men dug a tunnel from a nearby sewer to access the vault—and his unusual flair. Spaggiari would write a book about the theft titled *Fric-Frac*, recounting that his crew set up a special dining area near the vault to nourish themselves with "liver pâté, fancy sausage, smoked ham, crates of fruit," and wine during their long weekend pilfering safe-deposit boxes inside the bank.

Spaggiari was arrested months later but escaped custody by jumping from a second-story magistrate's office during an interrogation. Authorities watched him being driven away on a motorcycle and never saw him alive again.

David lacked the style of Spaggiari. But his take was nearly twice the Frenchman's. He also was far ahead of the legendary Willie Sutton, the best-known bank robber in the United States, who, when asked why he robbed banks, was said to have replied, "That's where the money is."

From the 1920s through the 1950s, Sutton robbed dozens of banks, usually disguised as either a police officer or a deliveryman. In total, he stole more than $2 million. He was polite with his victims, soothing them with a calm voice while he committed his crimes. But his cohorts occasionally betrayed him to police. He did multiple turns in prison, spending about half his adult life behind bars. In 1969, he became a free man and found work as a security consultant.

By a multiple of almost nine, David had exceeded Willie

Sutton's cash grabs in one act of boldness. Maybe, David hoped, others would talk about him with admiration. Maybe he would be known for his guts, for his brains, for his cagey mind.

The guts part seemed a certainty. Unlike the other thieves and robbers, David had pulled an inside job. He knew he would be a suspect right away. Inside jobs at banks and armored-car companies were not rare, but they were usually for much smaller amounts.

Bigger robberies had occurred abroad. In 1976, robbers stole an estimated $20 million to $50 million from safe-deposit boxes in Beirut at the British Bank of the Middle East. In Italy in 1984, five robbers with guns stole $21.8 million from Brink's Securmark in Rome.

Close to Home

Tammy Ghantt's prayers weren't being answered, but only ten miles away, Steve and Michele Chambers seemed on the verge of getting everything they wanted.

In his mobile home the night of the heist, Steve had told his cohorts to maintain their regular spending habits to avoid attracting attention. But the advice apparently didn't apply to him. Even before the heist, he and Michele had itched to move up, though not out of the general area. In mid-October, they planned their move into a $635,000 house in Gaston County, located in the gated community of Cramer Mountain.

With millions of dollars, Steve and Michele obviously could've gone anywhere they wanted and as far from the crime scene as possible. But in a move that seemed baffling, they decided to stay close to home. Their new home was actually closer to the scene of the crime than their old one.

Their move to Gaston County, a twenty-minute drive from their mobile home in Lincoln County, seemed an odd choice.

Gaston County was the heart of North Carolina's remaining mill industry, hardly a destination place for the nouveau riche. And in the Charlotte area, Gaston's blue-collar sensibilities provided fodder for laughs at comedy clubs, where telling a performer you lived in Gaston meant a joke at your expense.

In the early 1900s, Gaston's textile industry had been so dominant that the county's economy was slow to diversify in later decades when textile plants faded and the rest of the area's economy modernized. Charlotte became a banking capital, while Gaston County stayed a center of mill culture. In 1995, more than one-third of the county's workers held jobs in manufacturing, twice the national average. Charlotte promoted itself as the latest glimmering city of the New South, and people there often derided Gaston residents as rednecks or lintheads, an epithet named for the white lint that stuck to mill workers' clothes and hair and followed them out of the mill.

Gaston's relatively slow economic pace gave many of its residents a certain wariness about the city just over the Catawba River. The Charlotteans were hardly insulted. Many avoided Gaston County except to drive through it, heading west on Interstate 85 into the scenic mountains of Asheville. Besides, they could learn all they cared to about Gaston from the news, which always seemed full of crime from the county.

Steve certainly didn't care about Gaston's reputation. He liked the area, had family around, and wanted to show the people he had grown up with, who knew him as a small-time operator, that now he was a big shot. The house purchase indicated he planned to live there for a long time, assuming the police never got hold of him.

⊱⊰

On a mid-October afternoon, Michele showed up at her parents' house in Mount Holly. "I have a surprise," she told her mom. "I wanna show you something, where I'm gonna be moving." Michele drove her mother and sister to Cramer Mountain, stopping at its security gate.

Michele was moving into a place with a security gate? Seems like one of her crazy escapades, her mother figured. Michele couldn't possibly afford a house there. But Michele parked in front of a swanky one, at 503 Stuart Ridge, and led them inside. Her mom, Sandra Floyd, was stunned. Alone with Michele in a bedroom, she said to her daughter, "*I* can't afford something like this. You tell me how *you* can."

Michele told her mother that she and Steve had saved up gambling winnings by keeping expenses low in their mobile home. Sandra replied that didn't seem like it would be enough. But Michele said the interior designers who owned the place had helped them with a great financing deal.

Sandra Floyd didn't know how to answer that. Not the type to delve too deeply into other people's finances, even her daughter's, she refrained from asking the terms of the mortgage or the amount of the down payment. She assumed Michele and Steve had paid around $100,000 down and secured a reasonable, affordable mortgage. That they might have acquired their money illegally was too unpleasant to seriously consider.

⊱⊰

Just because they made their new life close to home didn't mean Steve and Michele had relinquished travel. They didn't fly, because Steve hated planes, but on October 24, three weeks after the heist, they took a train to New York with Eric Payne and his wife, Amy. Steve came prepared, hauling $400,000 in cash, having gotten his cousin Nathan to remove it from a storage locker for him. Steve didn't know that Nathan also swiped $6,000 for himself.

Eric Payne had been making good use of the money that Steve paid him the night of the theft. Since then, Steve had given him about $200,000 more. On October 11, he rented a new Cadillac. He kept the car for nine days. Now, he was considering replacing his two-year-old pickup truck and also buying a motorcycle, a Harley-Davidson.

Eric and Steve didn't discuss the heist much on the trip. They went shopping with their wives in Manhattan, traveling in a white limousine that Steve paid $1,000 to rent. After Michele bought a brown Armani suit for $2,700 at Bloomingdale's, the limousine shuttled them to FAO Schwarz, the toy store on Fifth Avenue. They walked wide-eyed through the merchandise, with Michele going gaga over the Barbie display. She bought an antique Barbie for herself and remote-control cars for her children.

Then they were driven to New Jersey, south on the Garden State Parkway to Atlantic City. Steve tipped the limo driver $1,000 when they arrived. At the casino, Michele, a poker fiend, spelled out her strategy for her friends, insisting she wouldn't be one of those people who gave her winnings back to the casino. This strategy entailed actually winning something first, which she managed to do. Then she put her money where her mouth was, walking away with a $10,000 gain.

Of course, for the Chamberses these days, an extra ten grand wasn't a big deal. Steve had $400,000 with him. The first night, he lost $12,000 playing blackjack, a game for which his great poker face was worthless. But the next night he won big and drank so much Budweiser that when he accidentally bumped into a man on the boardwalk, he handed him a few thousand dollars.

Overall, the rich got richer. Steve came away winning $60,000, paid out largely in hundred-dollar bills. Their eleven-hour train trip home felt like a victory lap.

Steve and Michele's house closing was scheduled for October 27, right after their return. The couple arrived at the office of their attorney, Jeff Guller, about 2:00 p.m. that day. Steve brought $53,000 worth of money orders and two black bags packed with $430,000 in cash, all in twenties. Sitting across the table from Guller, Steve unzipped one of the bags to show him it was full of money.

Guller didn't act surprised to see the cash, despite having represented Steve on the worthless-check charges, an infraction suggesting that Steve was low on legitimate funds and could obtain large amounts only through scheming. As an attorney, Guller was not supposed to knowingly help clients get away with crimes. But he had about two hundred clients at a time, and he didn't always remember the details of their cases. When he asked Steve where the money came from, Steve said he'd won a lot of it gambling in Atlantic City.

Days earlier, Guller had told Steve and Michele that if they were going to use that amount of cash to buy the house, they would have to fill out forms reporting the source of the money. For obvious reasons, Steve didn't want to do that. Another possibility, Guller said, was securing checks for the transaction. They could still close on the $635,000 house as scheduled, but they would need those checks in the next week or so.

At the closing, Steve and Michele agreed to pay almost two-thirds up front. The sellers, their attorney, and two real-estate agents were also present. Steve and Michele didn't talk much during the fifteen-minute meeting. They signed the deed of trust.

The sellers, interior decorators named Sally Stowe Abernathy and J. R. Abernathy, were told that their buyers could afford a $433,000 down payment because Steve owned a string of Laundromats and had played in the NFL. The Abernathys had agreed to finance the remaining amount at $8,860 a month for two years. The Abernathys were profiting handsomely, having bought the home just two years earlier for $485,000. In an outside agreement, Steve and Michele would pay them about $40,000 in cash for furniture Michele liked that they had left in the house.

After the closing, Steve asked Guller if he could leave the two bags of cash in his law office for the time being. Guller said yes—a decision that would haunt him—but added that if Steve didn't come through with the checks, and soon, the cash would have to be used for the deal. Steve was confident he could get the checks on time and thought Guller's office was as good a place as any to store the cash. And he figured that although Guller probably knew he had lived in a mobile home, he didn't have to worry that the lawyer would call the police or get him in trouble. After all, he hadn't told Guller where the money came from, and he figured the lawyer wouldn't ask the wrong questions. He figured Guller's office assistants would keep quiet as well.

Steve began asking Guller about other ways to disburse money. Guller told him that keeping cash deposits to under $10,000 wouldn't typically oblige banks to file mandatory reports with the government. Guller, who sensed that Chambers either was a hood or just wanted to be seen as one, figured it wasn't a problem to tell a client how the government worked.

It wasn't the first time Steve had asked Guller this type of question. Steve once asked if a person could be indicted for simply lending money to criminals if he didn't know what the debtors were using it for. Not knowing what Steve was talking about, Guller had responded that as long as Steve didn't know, he was probably okay.

Steve's lawyer was well-known in the community, having served leadership roles with the Gaston County March of Dimes, the Red Cross, the Young Lawyers Association, and his synagogue. Years earlier, playing football for East Mecklenburg High School on the other side of the Catawba River, in Charlotte, the five-foot-seven center and linebacker had won all-conference honors.

But a relative's health issues had contributed to debt problems, and Guller's practice had been in trouble with the law and under the scrutiny of the state bar association. In 1989, his second wife pleaded guilty to embezzling from escrow accounts that clients had established with his practice. The state bar association ruled that Guller was indirectly responsible, allowing that he didn't know about the theft. He remained a practicing attorney with a reputation for combativeness in favor of his clients.

Steve now had a $433,000 challenge. He had to secure that amount in checks or money orders for the down payment. His game plan was to pay people he knew to get the checks for him. Steve would "lend" them briefcases of cash, from which the helpers would buy him money orders or cashier's checks that he could use for the house purchase. For their troubles, the helpers would get from 5 to 10 percent of the check amounts, in cash.

As part of these house-purchasing efforts came one of Steve and Michele's most startling cash indiscretions, which easily dwarfed Michele's previous breach of bank etiquette. Days after the closing, Michele walked into the Wachovia Bank in Belmont with $200,000 in cash inside a briefcase. She had $150,000 in hundreds and the rest in fifties and twenties, and she asked the teller for an official bank check, payable to herself under her former married name, Shelley Harris. Naturally, the bank teller declined and afterward filed a suspicious activity report.

Then Steve and Michele drove an hour north to Salisbury, North Carolina, to a First Union National Bank. There they had an accommodating teller named Kim Goodman, who not only knew the Chamberses but was expecting their visit. She and her husband, Mike Goodman—a friend of Steve's—had previously agreed that she would accept their check transaction in return for $10,000 in cash, which Steve would give to Kim on her lunch break that day. She convinced her superiors the deal was legitimate and filed the necessary paperwork.

By the end of the first week of November, Steve also obtained a $100,000 check with help from a friend, Calvin Hodge, and an $80,000 cashier's check with help from Calvin's father, John Hodge. Steve, who claimed he needed their help because he didn't have a checking or savings account, was more discreet in these efforts. Days after the closing, he put $108,000 in a briefcase and hauled it to a Burger King in the small Gaston County town of Dallas, where Calvin Hodge, an ice-cream-truck driver, waited for him. Hodge had agreed to convert the cash into a check at his local bank. He would keep the extra $8,000 as a fee.

The checks and money orders went into Guller's escrow account at First Citizens Bank. On November 6, the money was used as the down payment. As a legal fee for handling the house closing, Steve paid Guller $1,000.

In the meantime, Steve had to deal with legal problems that predated the heist. On November 12, he pled guilty to forty-two counts of obtaining property by false pretenses, the charges in his old check-writing scheme. He avoided state prison, coming away with five years of probation, community service, restitution, and a small fine.

While discussing the case with Guller before the plea, Steve bragged that he was "pretty slick" to have gotten his false checks cashed before the law caught up to him.

"Not slick enough," Guller shot back. "You're not smart. You're a distinctive-looking guy. You're six feet tall, two hundred fifty or two hundred sixty pounds, with a beard. How are people not going to recognize you?"

Staying Close to Home

The Chamberses' new home certainly left an impression. Those who opened the front door and stepped into the foyer immediately saw a curved staircase adorned with a faux leopard-skin stair runner, which climbed above a Haddorff grand piano, a large beveled mirror with a leopard-fabric frame, and a bronze statue of a woman. To the left was the dining room, which had a bust of Caesar on a pedestal overlooking the fine china laid out on a polished wooden table.

From there, a right turn led into the huge kitchen festooned with a statue of a fat chef, a ceramic elephant, and oil paintings of a leopard and elephant. An open layout connected the kitchen to the living room, where a gas-log fireplace and wooden entertainment center were bedecked with trimmings that included a statue of a horse, a goose decoy, and prints of elephants. The bookends on their shelves were statuettes of female nudes.

The most stunning part of the house may have been the master bedroom, which was sunken six steps from the rest of the first floor and had a glass fireplace, a leather-padded headboard, and, in its private bathroom, a sunken whirlpool six feet in diameter, flanked by four fluted columns. If filling the tub would take too long, they could instead use the spacious, marbled walk-in shower.

Next to the master bedroom was the study, where a Baccarat crystal chandelier hung from the ceiling and a black-and-gold family crest was on the wall. Steve could conduct his business at a gorgeous eight-drawer desk and be comforted by the presence of a handmade Civil War chess set.

Downstairs, their well-furnished basement had a game room and wine cellar. To the right of the stairs was a glossy, black-tiled bar stocked with Corona and Coors Light. A clown-faced lava lamp sat on the bar, sometimes accompanied in the room by a cheap painting of Elvis on velvet. They hadn't bought the velvet Elvis themselves; it had been left there by the previous owners, interior decorators for whom it was a gag gift, not actual wall art.

The game-room walls also featured a framed print of Robert E. Lee and plaques commemorating Steve's supposed former team, the Dallas Cowboys. Guarding the pictures was a wooden cigar-store Indian that stood six feet tall. The jewel of the room was a pool table that cost just under ten grand. A door from the game room opened into the three-hundred-square-foot wine cellar, which had gold wallpapering and a brick floor.

Outside, Michele and Steve added a $10,000 fence, which gave them privacy and allowed their dogs—a basset hound named Dallas and a poodle named Ty Cobb—to safely play outside. The couple enjoyed the dogs and sometimes playfully addressed the poodle as "you little bastard," a moniker befitting the baseball legend of the early twentieth century for whom the pooch was named. Michele decided to discontinue the practice one day after hearing a toddler relative exclaim, "Ty Cobb, you wittle bastard!"

This was all quite a step up from their mobile home in rural Lincoln County, and while the leopard decor may have seemed out-of-place in their fancy neighborhood, they weren't regularly entertaining the types of people who would roll their eyes at it. Among the guests at Steve and Michele's first Halloween party as millionaires was Kelly Campbell, who purchased a Cleopatra costume for the event, only to be told at the last minute not to wear it because other guests wouldn't be dressing up. Kelly had become a frequent visitor to the house, playing pool and poker with Steve with fresh stacks of dollar bills.

Kelly, of course, had made the heist happen in the first place by prodding David to steal the money, but now she was playing a subordinate role to Steve. Steve was making all the decisions about where to hide cash and about who got what. Kelly didn't seem to protest much, believing Steve was "connected" and knew what he was doing to keep them out of trouble, and that the money was "up north" somewhere with his crooked bankers. She still had one-third of the loot coming to her, but she figured she wouldn't ask Steve for it until the FBI had left her alone for a longer period. After all, it had only been a few weeks since they interviewed her at her home about David.

She was fine with Steve in charge. Her main involvement now, besides spending small amounts of money, was in talking with Ghantt on the phone and then telling Steve what he said. Of course, she still had no intentions of moving to Mexico with

David, though she let him think she did—maybe in December, when things quieted down, she would say.

Telling David this kept him happy or at least would allay any suspicions he might harbor about them turning on him. After all, David hadn't received any money, and if he thought Kelly was bailing on the move to Mexico, he might put two and two together, realize his share of the money and his life were in danger, turn himself in, and call the cops on them. So she decided to let him think she was still interested.

In reality, she wanted to use her share to buy a new place of her own not far from her family. She even looked at a two-story home for sale in Bessemer City, in Gaston County, and also considered moving outside the county.

But unlike Steve, she didn't want David killed. She still viewed him as a friend, and she wasn't someone who looked to kill people who got in her way. To this point, she had managed to talk Steve out of consummating the murder plot, saying it wasn't necessary, though they had discussed various possibilities, including having David injected with Clorox. (The bleach would be fatal, they figured.) David, of course, had no clue his murder was being considered.

The Halloween party was a low-key affair. Kelly, Steve, Michele, Eric and Amy Payne, and a few others talked with each other, sipped their beers, and listened to music. At one point, Steve took Kelly aside and turned the subject to the murder plan. If they didn't move forward, Ghantt was bound to lead the FBI back to the rest of them. Kelly was high and finally gave in.

"Just do whatever you need to do," she told Steve.

✻

An occasional presence at the house was Amy Grigg, the fiancée of Steve's cousin Nathan Grant. She was supposed to keep an eye on the money at Lincoln Self Storage. In early November, the company sent her a letter saying that if she did not pay the monthly fee, it would open the locker and sell the contents. Amy asked her mother, Kathy, to go pay the bill. Kathy did so and brought home the receipt.

Early November brought another important new house guest when Mike McKinney, the original bearer of the ID that David was now using, flew in from Illinois. Weeks earlier, McKinney had accepted Steve's offer of $250,000 to kill someone. When McKinney arrived, Steve told him the target was a man who was hiding in Mexico. Steve would pay one-half up front. He didn't say where he'd gotten all this money, and McKinney didn't ask.

McKinney had never been a hit man before. In fact, he didn't have a criminal record for *any* violence. He had been a smart, popular student at his high school in Bridgeport, Illinois, graduating with a GPA over 3.2. Standing a slim six-foot-four and sporting a close-cut brown beard, he had joined the marines after some community college and became a TOW gunner, able to fire antitank missiles.

McKinney repeated his willingness to accept Steve's offer. The amount of money impressed him enough that he ignored the danger associated with it. He learned he would have to travel to Mexico to deal with the target, known to him only as Scott, and that Scott would be under the impression that McKinney was giving him money. McKinney would take along cash in case no opportunity arose to kill Scott. In that case, he would give Scott money so Scott would trust his intentions and meet with him on future visits, when McKinney, of course, would again look for opportunities to kill him.

⋈

A few evenings later, after a meal, Michele and Steve were driving down Charlotte's Independence Boulevard when Michele spotted a sporty, white BMW passing them. "Look at that," she said to Steve. "Isn't that cute?"

"Yeah, it's okay," Steve said.

The car was a BMW Z-3 roadster, a convertible.

A few days later, while on another drive down Independence Boulevard, Steve turned into the BMW dealership. He said to his wife, "Do you want to drive one?"

She took it for a test drive down Independence. It felt good. Very good. It cost $27,000, and they paid for it in cash.

⋈

Looking for another way to hide or launder his money, Steve bought a furniture business located in downtown Gastonia, across the street from the county courthouse. The seller was an acquaintance of Steve's named Michael Staley, who had run the store as a discount outlet. Staley wanted $75,000 for the store, and when Steve declined that price, they agreed on $25,000 up front and an undetermined amount later. They wrote nothing down about future payments. Staley was recovering from stomach surgery and wanted as little trouble from the transaction as possible. He just wanted to close the deal.

Steve changed the store's name from Furniture Discount Center to M&S Furniture, for Michele and Steve, and closed it down temporarily to lay a new concrete floor and carpet, and to redo the bathroom. He also replaced the discount inventory with higher-end merchandise. Michele drove to area newspapers to buy ads for the new store and even purchased radio spots on a local station.

Meanwhile, Kelly Campbell was enjoying her new riches for the most part. No, she had not received anywhere close to one-third of the stolen money, but she had seen six figures. For the first time in her life, she could buy things without worrying about a budget. Her once-minuscule bank account at the AT&T Family Federal Credit Union was growing too. She had deposited $800 two days after the heist and $1,715 a week later. And she was thinking about buying a minivan.

Yet the FBI's visit to her home soon after the heist still had her nervous a month later in early November. When she decided to buy the minivan, she asked Steve to come with her and register it under a different name so it wouldn't draw unwanted attention.

It was November 13 when Steve and Kelly drove to the Harrelson Toyota dealership in Fort Mill, South Carolina, just south of Charlotte. They had $16,000 worth of twenty-dollar bills with them. Steve introduced himself to the salesman as Robert Dean Wilson, an alias he had used before for his check-writing scheme, and they agreed on terms for a Sienna XLE minivan. The paperwork required a social security number for Robert Dean Wilson, so Steve made one up off the top of his head. On the loan application, he put down his place of employment as Chambers Industries. A few days later, Kelly and Steve returned to the dealership to pay off the rest of the minivan with $14,220 in twenty-dollar bills.

A week later, for Thanksgiving, both sets of spouses—Kelly and Jimmy and Steve and Michele—drove together to Atlantic City for a few days of fun. It was Steve's second trip there in a month. Jimmy Campbell still didn't know what his wife had been involved in.

When they arrived in New Jersey, they did the Atlantic City thing, gambling, strolling the boardwalk, and shopping. Kelly bought leather coats for both herself and Jimmy and shopped at a Warner Brothers store for her children. Steve gave a hundred-dollar chip to a drink server as a tip.

In their room at the Hilton Hotel, Jimmy noticed Kelly unzip a duffel bag full of cash. She told him Steve and Michele had a bag just like it. He nervously asked his wife if the money was from the Loomis Fargo theft.

Though she could've hidden her involvement better if she wanted, it had been a stretch for Kelly to think she could keep her husband out of the loop in the first place. She finally told him the truth. He had figured as much, he said. Getting mixed up in this would change his life, and he was smart enough to be worried. Unfortunately, at the moment he was in no position to protest much, because Steve and Michele were his ride back to North Carolina.

Tercel to BMW

Loomis Fargo wanted to make somebody else rich—but this time on the company's own terms. Soon after the heist, Loomis posted a $500,000 reward for information leading to an arrest or conviction in the case, hoping it might produce a real lead in an investigation threatening to go cold fast. In mid-November, the company still held out hope a tip would produce results about David Ghantt's location.

Loomis, Fargo & Co. was formed in 1996 when Borg-Warner Security Corporation of Chicago, which owned a company called Wells Fargo Armored Services, merged with Wingate Partners of Dallas, which owned Loomis Armored. The new company, which employed 8,500 people, was owned 51 percent by Loomis shareholders and 49 percent by Borg-Warner Security.

The roots of the armored-transport industry date to the mid-nineteenth century and the California gold rush, when successful prospecting companies relied on horse-drawn carriages to safely transport gold. With the rise of railroads later in the century, trains became the favored way to move cash.

According to *Heists: Swindlers, Stickups, and Robberies that Shocked the World* by Sean P. Steele, modern practices date to the 1920s, when Brink's Express—now called Brink's Inc. and the largest armored-transport company in the United States, but back then a freight company—leased a school bus fortified with steel to Chicago companies transporting large amounts of cash. The idea caught on. Armored vehicles were faster and safer than the armed couriers then working in cities, and they were less vulnerable to robberies than trains.

Demand for armored cars increased dramatically after World War II, when the mass suburbanization of the United States led to more openings of banks outside of cities. Decades later, the large armored-car companies were transporting hundreds of millions of dollars each day. Still, they operated with slim profit margins because banks—which comprise much of their business—did not pay the companies any more than they had to. That was partially because bank officials cared little about who transported their cash as long as the movement was insured, which it was, by the armored-car companies themselves.

Loomis Fargo's announcement about its reward, combined with the coverage on *America's Most Wanted* (the network had replayed the Ghantt segment to make up for the ball-game snafu), had led to a barrage of tips, but none panned out. Many of the leads seemed inspired by non-heist-related pettiness. *He just bought a BMW, and his last car was a Tercel!* The agents had to check them out, but it was so easy to relay minor suspicions to the FBI that the bureau seemed overwhelmed with meaningless tips.

Then came a needle in the haystack. In the last days of October, a legal assistant from Jeff Guller's office called and told the hot line operator that a man named Steve Chambers had an extremely large amount of cash stashed in her employer's office and that it seemed suspicious, given the heist. The *America's Most Wanted* operator replied that they were not looking for anybody named Steve Chambers. That was the end of it.

Meanwhile, the FBI had received permission from a federal judge to monitor the telephone lines of Kelly Campbell, Tammy Ghantt, and Nancy Ghantt, David's sister. The phone-monitoring devices, called "pen registers," revealed the length of calls in progress as well as who called whom. Pen registers don't involve recording phone calls; that's the province of wiretaps, considered much larger infringements on citizens' privacy and thus harder for the FBI to gain permission to use. To have a judge allow a wiretap in this case, the FBI would need much more evidence and demonstrate that agents already had exhausted less intrusive approaches.

The judge's order gave the FBI permission to place pen registers on the phone numbers for two months. Meanwhile, the U.S. attorney's office subpoenaed toll records, which show records of past calls—who made them and how long they lasted.

The toll records indicated that Kelly Campbell had lied, that the numbers registered to Campbell and David Ghantt had telephone contact on October 3 and October 4, the day of the heist. Campbell had told the agents she hadn't talked to Ghantt for at least two or three weeks before the theft. They also began to suspect she'd been lying when she told them she and David smoked marijuana together. Loomis officials had since told the FBI that Ghantt passed his company drug tests.

Halloween came and went without any breaks in the case. Then, in the second week of November, the publicity began bearing fruit. An anonymous caller told the FBI she knew a woman named Michele Chambers who had just moved into an expensive house she shouldn't have been able to afford.

A few days later, on November 12, the FBI received another intriguing call about Chambers and her husband, Steve. The anonymous caller said that the couple had been living in a mobile home in Lincoln County until two weeks earlier, and that Steve and Michele had just bought a large, expensive house at the exclusive Cramer Mountain gated community in Gaston County.

The caller had no proof that they were involved in the heist, but the whole thing seemed suspicious because neither Steve nor Michele held a steady job. Steve was just a small-time crook who had been involved in holding stolen property, the caller said. When the caller had asked Michele how they could buy such a big house, Michele had beaten around the bush, saying that the seller and an attorney were taking care of things.

None of which proved, of course, that Steve Chambers was involved in the heist. His newfound cash could have been drug money or gambling winnings, or who knows what. But the feds planned to keep an eye on him. The supervisors assigned John Wydra to check out the Chamberses and their house purchase, figuring Wydra's experience investigating money laundering and financial transactions would be helpful.

Wydra drove from Charlotte to Gastonia, where the Gaston County Courthouse sat downtown across the street from a barbershop and a furniture store, to check the deed for the house transaction. As he walked up the steps of the courthouse, Wydra was unaware that Steve and Michele Chambers were starting up their furniture business a few hundred feet away.

Inside the courthouse, records showed that Steve and Michele's new house cost $635,000 and that they had paid most of it down, needing a loan for less than $200,000 of the purchase price. Wydra also researched their criminal records and learned of Steve's guilty pleas for obtaining property by false pretenses. The records on his case included a series of aliases he had used for the scams, and Wydra punched these into the FBI's database. They were names that wouldn't ordinarily turn heads—Robert Dean Wilson, Steven Jeffcoat. The case record showed Chambers was a scam artist and small-time crook, not someone capable or even interested in a crime of this magnitude.

But on November 18, the FBI received another confidential call that stood out. It was about a man named Eric Payne. According to the caller, Payne had gone on vacation for two weeks, starting the day after the heist, and was now spending more money than he should've been able to afford on his salary. He had just bought a new Chevy Tahoe and had explained his new wealth as an inheritance. Plus, the informant said, he worked at Reynolds & Reynolds, located less than a mile from the wooded area where the Loomis van had been found two days after the theft.

Agent Dick Womble dealt with this call. First, he checked records to see if any of Payne's relatives had recently died. None had, so the excuse about the inheritance seemed sketchy. Womble also drove to Reynolds & Reynolds and spoke discreetly with officials there. He learned that Payne had attended East Gaston High School and that Steve Chambers had briefly worked at Reynolds & Reynolds, years earlier when it was under different ownership.

The FBI now knew that Steve Chambers and Eric Payne, independently, were spending a lot of money. But the agents had no solid way to tie them together—besides knowing both had worked at Reynolds & Reynolds and attended East Gaston High School—or to tie them to David Ghantt or Kelly Campbell. The agents didn't even know if Chambers and Payne were spending Loomis money. The proximity of Payne's workplace to the van seemed a possible indication of something, but it could've been a coincidence.

A link between the suspects, if only a minor one, came when agents obtained permission to include Steve Chambers's phone numbers in the pen registers and toll records. They noticed continued phone contact between Payne and Chambers, and also that Jeff Guller, the attorney who had called them the week after the heist about Kelly Campbell's refusal to take a polygraph, had had phone contact with Chambers the next day. Maybe Chambers and Campbell knew each other, though that was uncertain. The connection was nothing to seek an arrest warrant on, but for the first time the FBI had a way to link Steve Chambers to Kelly Campbell.

The agents cross-checked every new name with the monthly reports of the Financial Crimes Enforcement Network, a bureau of the U.S. Treasury Department that coordinates information in suspicious activity reports filed by banks nationwide. The FBI hoped Kelly Campbell, Steve Chambers, or Eric Payne would show up on its compiled list, but since the reports often took two or three months to weave through official channels to the FBI, that hadn't yet happened. A report taken in October usually wouldn't reach agents until mid-December or later.

Connecting Steve Chambers to Kelly Campbell, however tenuous the link, seemed like an important step. After all, Campbell had been on the phone with Ghantt the day of the crime and had lied about it to the FBI. And despite all the informants and interviews, the FBI still had no clue if David Ghantt was dead or alive. And if he was alive, the agents had no idea where he might be. Idaho? Mexico? Venezuela? He could've been anywhere, even in Charlotte.

Anxious for a new approach around Thanksgiving, the FBI engaged the inexact science of behavior profiling. Dick Womble and Mark Rozzi drove from Charlotte to Stafford, Virginia, to the FBI's National Center for Analysis of Violent Crimes. The behavioral analysis unit there focused on finding serial killers, rapists, and kidnappers, stockpiling databases and tips from crimes across the country that helped it devise theories about where fugitives with similar backgrounds might have gone. David Ghantt didn't fit the bill of what the unit normally studied, but Womble and Rozzi figured the experts' eyes wouldn't hurt. They had already discussed the case with the unit's experts over the phone, but they wanted to talk with them in person.

Womble and Rozzi told the people there everything they'd learned about Ghantt and his family. They mentioned that his relatives and friends said he liked reading about counterintelligence and the FBI. They mentioned his coworkers said he'd complained about his marriage and suspected an affair between him and Kelly Campbell. They disclosed that the coworkers said Ghantt had frequently criticized Philip Johnson—the man who had pulled off the bigger heist in Jacksonville—and would say things like, "Where that guy screwed up was, he stuck around. He should've cut all ties."

The unit's experts processed the information. Ghantt's physical build suggested he probably couldn't have moved all the money by himself and that he probably needed help with the crime, the experts told Rozzi and Womble. Many of Ghantt's favorite novels had plots with spies fleeing to Central and South America, so perhaps he was somewhere there, trying to live the fascinating life of one of the characters and avoiding Philip Johnson's error. And yes, Ghantt's marital history gave reason to suspect that another woman was involved, the experts said.

The conclusions seemed simple to have come from behavior-profiling experts, and they seemed similar to what agents had already surmised. But Rozzi and Womble were glad that the bureau had drawn reasonable preliminary conclusions and seemed on the right track.

Meanwhile, Kelly Campbell remained the target of periodic physical surveillance, which revealed in mid-December that she was driving a new Toyota minivan. Agents jotted down the license plate number, which allowed them to start tracking the purchase and registration information.

Womble and Rozzi, back in Charlotte from Virginia, tried their luck again on Campbell, calling her on December 29 to set up another meeting nearly three months after their previous one. They wanted to talk with her about Ghantt and ask her again to sit for a lie-detector test. Campbell was busy that morning but was available to meet in the afternoon at the Gaston Mall.

Once there, they sat down over coffee, making small talk about Kelly's son, who was recovering from appendicitis. Then they got down to business.

"We're still trying to locate David Ghantt," Womble told her.

Kelly stayed true to her prior story, saying she had no idea where he was. During their fifteen minutes together at the mall, Kelly's cell phone and pager were ringing and buzzing almost constantly, but she didn't respond to them. Womble and Rozzi managed to hide their wonder at this. They also concealed their own knowledge, developed through the toll records, that she had previously lied concerning her contact with Ghantt before the heist.

"We think there's more to this than you're telling us," Womble said. "Would you take a polygraph for us?"

She told them to call her attorney, Jeff Guller, with their questions. They shook hands with her and she left. Neither agent believed she would ever agree to take the polygraph.

><

On December 28, a man placed a call to the FBI with information about Steve Chambers. He said he had never met him but that he knew a guy named Mike Staley, who had sold Chambers his furniture store in Gastonia. The caller had talked with Staley, who told him he had been inside Steve's new house and had seen a bag so heavy with twenty-dollar bills that Steve had trouble lifting it. The caller suspected Chambers was in on the heist. For the FBI, this was another tip that something was awry with Chambers.

By the end of 1997, nearly three full months into the investigation, the FBI had used phone and car registration records to connect three important suspects. Campbell had been shown by phone records to have lied about her contact with David Ghantt on the day of the crime, and her lawyer had telephone contact with Steve Chambers the day after having called the FBI on her behalf.

At the same time, agents had no reliable leads on David Ghantt's location and no firm sense of whether he was alive or dead.

Dead Man in Mexico?

The international fugitive could last only so long on $25,000. His heady October days of lobster, parasailing, and fancy hotels quickly ate away at David Ghantt's first heist installment. In the first week of November, he realized he needed more cash, and he wanted it fast. To his extreme displeasure, he had yet to receive his one-third share of the loot.

The man who pulled off a $17 million heist was thus reduced to eating homemade grilled cheese sandwiches and pasta, saving his money in case the next sum failed to arrive in a timely fashion. He was renting an apartment with a kitchen for about $800 a month, decorating the walls with Pittsburgh Steelers paraphernalia near Cancun's beach off Kukulkan Boulevard.

He wasn't alone. He had met a woman named Lindsey, who was twenty-four years old and Canadian, as far as David knew. He'd met her at Christine, his favorite hangout. As far as Lindsey knew, David was a small-time drug dealer from the States, and his name was not David, it was Mike McKinney. His shadiness did not bother her. Every so often, she somehow popped up with a wad of cash herself.

The Cancun couple drank at local clubs and went scuba diving; he had purchased $3,000 worth of diving equipment and a navigational device for $900 more. She moved in with him after getting kicked out of her own place in the middle of November. They hosted parties attended by her friends, who were Ecstasy dealers, and while David never indulged in their wares, he enjoyed their company.

Lindsey had a friend who worked for a car-rental company, and one day David and his girlfriend rented a Volkswagen Beetle to go driving outside Cancun, blowing the speed limit and then some. It was hardly his most serious transgression of the year. Still, a local police officer's siren blared behind them.

As they were stopped on the side of the road, David was confident his Michael McKinney ID would stand up to scrutiny. Nobody had given him trouble over it yet. He rolled down his window as the officer walked up to the car.

"It's very hot today, sir," the officer said. "I'd like a drink."

David had heard about the police in Cancun and knew exactly what to do. Without a word, he placed sixty dollars in the ticket book the officer was holding out to him.

"Have a nice day," the officer said. He drove away and left them to enjoy themselves, never even checking the ID.

The Cancun fling with Lindsey was only so fulfilling. From a pay phone, David called Kelly Campbell on Tuesdays using a calling card and demanded the first installment of the rest of his money. He wanted fifty grand as soon as possible, he told her.

Kelly relayed his words to Steve, who had her tell David they would send a man answering to Bruno to Cancun with cash for him. She relayed this to David, who suggested they meet at the Rainforest Café in Cancun.

Back in North Carolina, the hit man's trip to Mexico almost ended before it began. The real Mike McKinney, a.k.a. Bruno, was not an especially good smuggler. In the men's bathroom at Charlotte Douglas International Airport, he bundled the $10,000 given to him by Steve inside the waist of his jeans and prepared to walk through the metal detector. As he exited the bathroom, though, the money began falling down his pants! He scurried back inside, his heart stopping as he envisioned airport security swarming around him.

Luck was on his side. The money stayed above his ankles. He readjusted the cash into more manageable stacks and walked as confidently through the metal detector as he could.

When his plane landed in Cancun, McKinney booked a room at the Mex Hotel and went to the Rainforest Café for the appointment with "Scott," who he knew was using his identification papers. He was under the impression Scott was hiding in Mexico because he shot somebody; that's what Steve had told him.

But McKinney couldn't find his target. He scanned the Rainforest Café, a safari-themed restaurant with a jungle motif. He was looking for a man who, he had been told, was six feet tall with red or blond hair and weighed between one hundred thirty and one hundred sixty pounds. McKinney knew little else about him, having never even seen a picture. Ghantt was actually there, but McKinney couldn't find him. McKinney left, came back later, and still couldn't locate his man.

Around town, he asked people who spoke English if they knew anyone named Mike. Not surprisingly, no one knew who he was talking about.

It wasn't a total loss though. Unable to make the delivery, the aspiring hit man decided to turn his time abroad into a drunken escapade and spending spree. First, McKinney bought T-shirts and shorts, having arrived only with long-sleeved tops and pants. Then he went out drinking and meeting women, drinking and Jet Skiing, drinking and sunbathing, and then meeting more women. He visited Cancun bars like Dady Rock, where the dancing got pretty wild, and La Boom, where he enjoyed the bikini contests.

He called Steve and said he was having no luck. Steve told him to fly back to North Carolina so they could regroup. McKinney would catch a flight the next day, after one more night on the town. He would be returning to Cancun soon enough.

While McKinney was getting piss drunk, David was getting pissed off. The man with the tan from a can wanted his money. On the phone, relaying his anger that Bruno couldn't find him at the Rainforest Café, he told Kelly to have him bring it to a room at the Villa Marlin beachfront complex of apartments and condominiums, which David had rented just for this contact. He didn't want anybody up north to know where he was really living, in case they got arrested. Little did he know that McKinney had already flown back to the States.

A few days later McKinney returned to Cancun, again with instructions to kill, if possible. This time, he made it through the airport's metal detector like a pro, having more skillfully bundled the $10,000 in five stacks of twenties. He knew from Steve Chambers to go to room 202 of the Villa Marlin.

At 6:00 a.m. on this mid-November morning, McKinney knocked on the door of room 202. A woman answered who didn't speak English. It was clear his man wasn't inside. He had the wrong room.

He called Steve, who had made a mistake; he'd meant to say room 206. He told McKinney to try again. For reasons he didn't explain, Steve also called off the murder plan for now and told McKinney to wait until the next morning to make the delivery. That night, McKinney spent more than $1,000 of the money meant for his target.

At 5:30 a.m. the next day, McKinney knocked on the correct door. David opened it. McKinney asked, "You lookin' for help from Charlotte?"

David let him in, and McKinney dropped $8,500 on David's bed, all in twenties. David was furious. "That's it? That's it? What the fuck is this? There's nothing else?"

"That's all they gave me," McKinney said.

David said he'd wanted fifty grand.

"This is what they gave me. This is what you get," McKinney said. Before he left, he explained that he had been given the wrong room the previous day.

"Yeah, that's par for the course," David said with disgust as McKinney turned and left.

David was stunned. At this pace, it would take more than five hundred separate cash deliveries for him to get his $5 million. Within minutes of Bruno's departure, he realized for the first time that he might never see his share of the stolen millions. He lay on his bed staring at the ceiling, straining to give his cohorts up north the benefit of the doubt. Maybe complications had arisen that he didn't know about. Maybe they would send more next time.

><

Frustrations aside, he no longer had to watch his wallet. He was still worried about getting his money, but at least he had enough to eat out now.

A week after this first cash delivery, Bruno came to Cancun again, this time meeting David in a hotel restaurant. Under a table, Bruno slipped him a brown paper bag and left. David finished his meal, returned to his room, and opened the bag. There was only $8,500 inside. "What the hell is this?" he shouted.

He paged Kelly to let her know he would be calling. He yelled at her on the phone: "What the hell is this shit?"

Kelly asked, "Did you get your money?"

"Yeah, I did," David said. "I got eight grand. I wanted eighty."

Kelly said she would speak to Steve about it.

David again hoped for the best, that he would start receiving his millions if he waited just a little longer. In the meantime, he tried again to persuade Kelly to move down there sooner rather than later. He told her he loved her and wanted to see her. She told him she was worried the FBI was tracking her. It was too soon.

He demanded again that she and the others send him more money, for their benefit as well as his. He had thought about it, and they could all invest in a Jet Ski operation. He said he had already talked to a Mexican lawyer about setting up a rental business. They would need about $80,000 to begin, and then they could live off the fees.

"This company can send you all a big check every month," he claimed.

Charlotte's nightlife is far, far tamer than Cancun's, but you wouldn't have known that from following McKinney around. Between his trips to Mexico, McKinney's evenings in North Carolina were spent little differently than his time in Cancun. He made the city's downtown, which is actually called "uptown," his home away from home, becoming a short-time regular at its hot spots. If the hour was late and he lacked female companionship, he sometimes headed to the Paper Doll Lounge, a strip joint in another part of the city. Most nights or mornings he returned to his hotel room in Gastonia or Charlotte, where he waited to talk to Steve about his upcoming travels to Mexico. Before each trip, they agreed that McKinney would try to kill David if the circumstance presented itself. If it didn't, McKinney would continue to give him money and maintain his trust until killing him became feasible on some future trip.

≍

One evening in early December, David's view of Cancun as a safe haven came to an abrupt halt.

He was eating dinner at the Hard Rock Café, watching rock videos on a mounted screen and catching glimpses of the beach. Then, to his dismay, another customer approached his table and said he recognized him.

"Hey, man," the stranger said, "you look like that guy from North Carolina who stole like twenty million dollars."

Inside, David froze. "That's cool," he said. "But my name's Mike."

The stranger returned to his table, oblivious to David's worst panic attack since he had been in Mexico. He finished his meal in a daze, paid his check, and returned to his apartment.

He got Kelly on the phone and told her what just happened. "I gotta get out of here," he said.

She told him they would send Bruno back and think of another plan for him. Steve would arrange to have him moved to Brazil or somewhere else, she said.

Meanwhile, David began staying in his apartment all day and night, scared he'd be recognized if he ventured out. Then, a few days later, he decided to get a room at a Holiday Inn. He'd begun worrying that reward-seekers were on his trail and thought that moving from hotel to hotel could keep them at bay.

About a week before Christmas, and just after the Hard Rock Café sighting, Bruno called David at the hotel. He said he had more money and that he was going to help David move. The two met at a hotel at Calinda Beach, where Bruno told David the plan was to move him to Mexico City and then maybe to Brazil. It seemed like a smart idea to David, who knew he had to leave Cancun.

Back in his rented apartment, David explained to Lindsey that he had to go to Cozumel for a few days. He took some clothes and the Ray-Ban sunglasses with him, leaving behind the expensive scuba equipment, a CD player, pots, pans, and about $15,000 in cash that he had stocked there in case more money from the States didn't arrive.

Then he and Bruno took a forty-five-minute cab ride south on Route 307, a four-lane highway, to the tamer resort area of Playa del Carmen, a former fishing town that had grown popular when Cancun became a tourist destination in the 1970s. On the cab ride, David asked in a quiet, shaky voice if Bruno knew who he was. Bruno said no, and that he couldn't care less.

Once in Playa del Carmen, they took a ferry to the resort island of Cozumel, known worldwide for its fantastic diving. Booking a room at the plush, four-star Presidente Hotel, where rates started at about $310 a night, they went inside, sat on the balcony, and poured themselves drinks.

"I used to be a truck driver," David told Bruno. "I'm doing pretty good for myself, huh?"

McKinney nodded. As far as he knew, David was just an ordinary schlub on the run from a shooting in the States that no one had ever heard of.

But then David then proceeded to tell him how exactly he'd

wound up in Mexico. "I hit it for fourteen million dollars," David said.

As David told the story, McKinney noticed his voice filling with confidence. McKinney was simultaneously impressed with David and terrified for himself. This wasn't some nondescript drug-related shooting he'd been dealing with. It was a candidate for Crime of the Year, which meant it had FBI written all over it. Until this conversation, McKinney had figured this little job presented little danger to his freedom. And while he hadn't previously heard of the Loomis Fargo heist, after hearing David describe it, he realized there was a pretty good chance that everybody involved would get caught. And he thought to himself that Steve wasn't paying him enough.

McKinney hid his thoughts, and their discussion turned to how Americans on the lam could make a living in Mexico. David brought up the Jet Ski business. With a $75,000 to $80,000 investment, they could buy eight to ten Jet Skis, he said, and rent them out for eighty or ninety dollars an hour. There would be no need to ever return to America. It was just small talk, of course. David and McKinney weren't going into business together. They were both in Mexico for different reasons, and only one of them figured he had to stay.

McKinney then forgot who was paying his salary and told David that his cohorts were spending the money wildly in North Carolina, moving into a fancy new home and buying high-end vehicles. David wasn't surprised, but the details infuriated him. As the team member who actually stole the money, he believed he merited a standard of living at least as high as the others, and here he was relying on their bumbling attempts to get him $10,000 at a time.

As for McKinney, he didn't abandon the effort. He figured that maybe, just maybe, he could arrange for someone else to do the deed. Then McKinney could get his $250,000 from Steve and be on his merry way. He had recently hooked up with a local hoodlum named Robert, who worked a menial job in Cancun's tourism industry. He had asked Robert if he knew anyone who would kill for money. Robert said he could help.

Bruno said he was going to fly to Mexico City himself to find a place there for David to stay temporarily before the move to Brazil. Meanwhile, he said, David should return to Cancun and call Robert, who would get David a plane ticket to Mexico City. David had no idea he was in serious danger.

Luckily for David, he still had his Pittsburgh Steelers jersey. His love for the team may have saved his life.

At McKinney's word, David arranged to meet Robert at Señor Frog's in Playa del Carmen, a waterfront bar where tourists sip tropical drinks in eighteen-inch glasses. Robert, a six-foot-three, three-hundred-pound brute, was immediately drawn to David's football jersey, which had the name and number of running back Jerome Bettis.

"Man, where the hell did you get that jersey?" he asked. "I been looking all over for something like that!"

They talked sports over Dos Equis, chips, and salsa. David

gave Robert about $200 worth of pesos to buy him a one-way ticket to Mexico City, and Robert gave David a cell phone.

The next day, Robert called David to say he had bad news. The money had been stolen. "Come to Cancun to see me again," he said. "I'll put you up. I need to talk to you anyway."

David took a cab to Cancun and wound up meeting Robert's family. Then Robert took him aside.

"Man, I feel bad about what's gonna happen to you," he said. He explained that Bruno had tried to get one of Robert's henchmen to kill David. "What'd you do?" Robert asked.

"I'm a bank robber," David said.

"Man, you're in a bad way," Robert said. He said he liked David, a fellow Steelers fan, and felt guilty about being a player in a plot to kill him. He told David that Bruno was trying to lure him to an isolated place somewhere, maybe even in a jungle.

David was flabbergasted, and it showed on his face.

"What you really oughta do," Robert said, "is go right back to these people with a gun and kill them."

The suggestion didn't really help. How could David kill anyone? True, he had been in the army, but his job had been repairing helicopters.

"Keep your distance from Bruno," Robert told him. It was starting to make sense to David why the money was coming down in dribs and drabs. He felt he owed Robert for saving his life. He gave him $3,000 out of gratitude. In return, Robert set David up with a fake Mexican ID and birth certificate.

David wondered who else was in on this. He didn't suspect Kelly, thinking she was just a middle person. It was probably her friend Steve, who seemed to control all the money, at least according to what Bruno had said on the hotel balcony.

David called Kelly and asked if she still had the .45-caliber gun he'd left with her the night of the crime. He figured that with Steve around, she might need it.

And he figured he wouldn't see his share of the money without a fight.

Stolen Stolen Money

While David Ghantt worried in early December about getting his share of the loot in Mexico, Steve Chambers fretted in North Carolina over safeguarding the whole take.

This had become a serious problem, as more than $1 million had disappeared. His cousin Nathan Grant's fiancée, Amy Grigg, had a half brother named Jody Calloway. Jody, along with his wife Jennifer, had seen a receipt from Lincoln Self Storage lying around the Grigg home and schemed to steal from the locker after Amy mentioned they'd been hiding money for the mob there.

The first part of the Calloway scheme involved Jennifer renting her own locker at Lincoln Self Storage on November 22 so she could gain access past the facility's computer-keyboard security system. Jody then practiced working with a torch, and in the following days he would burn Nathan Grant's locker open and steal about $1.3 million. It was the hottest money around, having been stolen twice in the previous two months. Before he left, Jody replaced the damaged lock with a new, identical one that of course wouldn't work.

Nathan Grant and Amy Grigg had collected about $70,000 from Steve to keep watch over multiple lockers. When Amy checked on one and couldn't open it, she nervously informed Nathan, who checked it out himself a few days later. Amy was right, he discovered; the locker wouldn't open.

They panicked. Nathan bought a lubricant, hoping maybe the lock was frozen and needed something to loosen it up. He worried that if anything happened to the cash, Steve would think he stole it. Unaware that Jody had stolen the money, Amy told her half brother she was scared the mob might come after her.

Two weeks later, when Nathan tried again to open the locker, his key still didn't work. His face white as a ghost, he told Steve, and they drove together to the facility to examine it. They saw burn marks, and Steve figured somebody probably had cut their lock off and replaced it with an identical one. He talked to a woman who worked there, but she wasn't helpful. It wasn't her responsibility, she said. Steve had her call a locksmith, and when the lock was cut off, he opened the locker. It was completely empty. Half a dozen suitcases and four cardboard boxes, all placed there full of cash, were missing.

Nathan panicked. Steve didn't curse or yell, and he seemed to believe his cousin's remorse was sincere. He continued to lie to Nathan about the source of the money, saying he'd been holding it for others. "They're gonna kill me," Steve said. "I gotta go to Chicago and explain to them that it's gone."

Of course, Steve couldn't report this theft to the cops. All he could do was try to keep the rest of the cash in safer hands. First, he removed the money from the other storage lockers in the area. Then he enlisted his relatives and friends to help him store it in safe-deposit boxes in banks, which he felt were more secure.

The loss wouldn't land a rich man like Steve Chambers in the poorhouse. It wouldn't even threaten his $8,860 monthly mortgage payments. He could still afford to buy his old mobile-home property, using a $62,000 check he secured for a fee through John Hodge, who along with his son the ice-cream man had secured checks for the down payment on the $635,000 house. Steve then let Nathan and Amy live in his old home for $500 a month.

And he could still afford to pay his lawyer, Jeff Guller, a $10,000 fee for simply holding two briefcases in his office. These were the briefcases containing the $433,000 that Steve had planned to use to buy his new house, before Guller told him that paying with cash required filling out paperwork. Guller, whose office assistants almost immediately wondered if the cash was Loomis Fargo money, was reluctant to take a fee for holding the cash, but he relented when Steve, in the end, called it a Christmas gift.

After Thanksgiving, Steve asked Guller for his briefcases back. The lawyer returned them on consecutive Sunday mornings, November 30 and December 7, in a restaurant parking lot in Gastonia. When Guller returned the second briefcase, Steve asked if he had taken his $10,000. Guller said yes, he had.

⋈

Steve's decision to keep the money in safe-deposit boxes led him to sully the hands of people who were previously uninvolved in the heist.

On December 12, Steve and Michele invited relatives over to celebrate Michele's daughter's sixth birthday. At the Cinderella-themed party, as guests ate from deli trays and admired the three-tiered castle cake, Steve asked his father-in-law, Dennis Floyd, a truck driver, to come downstairs with him. They played pool on Steve's $10,000 table and made small talk before sitting down at the bar.

Steve said, "You know, we do a lot of gambling, and Michele tells me you're in a financial bind."

"If you drive a truck, you're always in a financial bind," Dennis Floyd replied.

Steve told his father-in-law he would give him $20,000 to store $1 million in cash. Dennis Floyd would need to sign up to manage a safe-deposit box—in his own name—in which Steve would hide the cash.

Dennis Floyd said he would do it.

Days later, Michele drove her BMW to her parents' house in Mount Holly to pick up her stepfather and drive them to a bank. She had $1 million in a briefcase.

She was wearing a silver raincoat. Her stepdad was wearing a black leather jacket. They were like Bonnie and Clyde, Michele thought. After Michele pulled into a parking space, they walked inside and cosigned for access to a safe-deposit box.

In the coming weeks, Steve would pay his in-laws another $20,000 to open more safe-deposit boxes that would hold another $900,000 of his "gambling money." In total, Dennis Floyd would rent seven boxes.

The Chamberses also asked Steve's parents to hide money and other items in safe-deposit boxes. When his parents asked why, they told Steve's mother they had won at gambling in Las Vegas and told his father they had important papers and jewels that needed extra security. Steve's parents then cosigned for three boxes, and Steve said he would help them with a down payment for a new home.

Steve also got friends in on the act. The best man at his wedding, David Craig, accepted $80,000 to open six safe-deposit boxes in his own name that would hold a total of $1.9 million. Steve told him the money belonged to a friend who needed it shipped somewhere. In addition, Calvin Hodge took $40,000 from Steve to open three safe-deposit boxes in his own name that would hold $900,000. He also rented a storage unit that held $770,000.

Steve involved his cousin Nathan Grant as well, asking him to cosign for a safe-deposit box with Amy Grigg. About $400,000 went inside.

Despite the theft from Lincoln Self Storage, Steve still trusted his cousin. He occasionally cracked, "You owe me $1.96 million," but only as a joke. Nathan and Amy, worried that whomever Steve had been holding the money for would come after them, told him they were scared, but he told them not to worry, that the people "up north" didn't know they were involved.

True, Steve and Michele had already set off alarm bells with their spending right after the heist, but when it came to managing the money, all had been going well to this point. But the Calloways' theft from the locker had changed everything, affecting how Steve did business and leading him to invite close friends and relatives, even his parents, into the mess he'd created. It would be a long time before Steve knew who had stolen his stolen money.

Even during the best of times, criminal multimillionaires have a lot on their minds. Several potential problems were gnawing at Steve. What would happen if David Ghantt decided to turn himself in? What if the murder plot went wrong? What was the best way to hide the money? He was nervous about all of these issues and more, and figured it made sense to use his old FBI contact to try to gauge the bureau's progress on the heist investigation. His season of brazen acts, one after the other, could hardly be topped by his initiating contact with the FBI a few months after the heist. He placed a Christmas call to the bureau's Charlotte office.

Steve asked for Phil King, the agent he had worked with when he was an informant. He claimed he just wanted to say hello, to find out how King was doing. Steve asked King if he was working on any special cases, hoping the answer would help him gauge the FBI's progress on the heist investigation.

Just the usual stuff, King said.

Steve wished him a Merry Christmas and jokingly asked, "Did you buy me a gift?"

King returned the sentiment and the joke. Then they hung up.

Christmas Bear

Steve and Michele had no qualms about inviting people outside their inner circle into their home. In mid-December 1997, Steve called an old friend with whom he had worked as a teenager at Belmont Hosiery, a sock factory where he'd also worked with Eric Payne. They had lost touch for about a decade afterward but reconnected in 1994 at a little-league baseball game. Steve invited the friend, who now worked as a printing-company manager, to his New Year's Eve party.

The friend, who lived in Belmont, told him he thought the drive to Lincoln County would be too far, at least forty-five minutes.

"Don't worry," Steve said. "I moved."

"Where to?"

"I live in Cramer Mountain now."

"Get outta town!"

The friend drove to see Steve before the New Year's Eve

party. The grand piano, the pool table, and the poker table all caught his eye. Steve told him that the place cost more than half a million dollars, and that he'd already paid most of it off.

"How the hell did you manage that?" the friend asked.

"It all comes from taking risks," Steve said.

"It looks like you're doing pretty good," the friend replied. "Can you get me hooked up?"

"I might have something for you," Steve said. The friend asked for a loan for $25,000 at 1 percent interest. When Steve would eventually offer him $100,000 to smuggle $2.5 million to the Cayman Islands, the friend responded that he would think about the deal and get back to him.

⋇

Another houseguest was Ruth Staley, mother of the previous owner of the Chamberses' furniture store. Steve and Michele liked Ruth Staley. One Friday in late December, they invited her and her three grandchildren to their house for pizza, saying they always bought pizza for their kids on Fridays to celebrate the end of the week.

Ruth accepted the invite, and the size of their house impressed her. During the visit, she noticed the barrels in the garage and commented favorably on their royal blue color. "What do you have in those?" she asked.

"Dog food," Michele said.

Meanwhile, Steve was keeping a close eye on Kelly Campbell. He wanted to make sure she didn't do anything to get them in trouble, and she remained a frequent guest at his house. Of course, compared to Steve, Kelly wasn't spending much at all. She had bought the new minivan, leather jackets, an all-terrain vehicle, and dirt bikes, and had just taken her kids to Disney World—the first time she'd ever flown in a plane. She was more or less following Steve's advice from the night of the crime, that everyone should lie low and hold off on big purchases. Still, some of her acquaintances had noticed she'd been spending more money than usual; she explained that she'd been selling pot.

She was still talking to David on the phone every week or so. During a December call, he told her he didn't want to meet Bruno anymore. He wouldn't say why, but he was insistent that somebody else deliver the cash to him. He clearly trusted her less than before.

When Kelly mentioned her recent trip to Florida with her kids, David revealed that he knew about the money being spent on houses and vehicles, and that he wasn't pleased, especially since he had seen less than $40,000 of the $17 million.

"Yeah, that's what Steve is doing," Kelly told him, "but I haven't bought anything but a van."

David would've been even more upset to hear of the extravagance of Eric Payne, Steve's last-minute recruit who had played no role in the planning but seemed to be outspending David by a large margin. Payne had bought a motorcycle, a pickup truck, a diamond necklace for his wife, Amy, and a computer for their daughter. Eric's family also went in for plastic surgery. His wife and two sisters had breast implants. Amy also got a nose job.

Of course, whatever the Paynes were spending was nothing

compared to Steve and Michele's activity. And while Kelly never complained to Steve about his extravagance, one day he volunteered to her, "I know you're probably thinking, here I am buying all these things, when I told y'all not to. But I got ways to make it look legitimate."

Kelly didn't argue with him. She took his word for it. But the FBI's late-December interview with her at the Gaston Mall had made her increasingly nervous that her connection to David would lead to her arrest. She worried that Jeff Guller, the attorney, had not done all he could to make the agents leave her alone.

Steve referred her to another Gastonia attorney he knew. Kelly told this lawyer the FBI wanted to polygraph her and paid the lawyer's firm $10,000 as a retainer. The lawyer set up a private lie-detector test administered by a retired FBI agent to see how she would do. She failed miserably.

Steve had hired this second lawyer for himself because he was upset with the plea bargain that Guller had arranged on his fraud case. He was considering buying a bar or a nightclub as a way to launder money, but the state wouldn't grant a liquor license to a convicted felon, so he needed his criminal record cleared. Steve wanted both lawyers, separately, to explore having his guilty plea overturned.

Santa Claus was flush with funds this year, so gift-giving time was the highlight of the Christmas party at 503 Stuart Ridge, where a twelve-foot tree loomed impressively over the guests and catering was provided by Boston Market—turkey, ham, and all the trimmings. The Chamberses were good at giving presents, and they didn't skimp.

Michele's grandfather Roy Willis received a small, wrapped box from Michele and Steve, who made sure their video camera caught his reaction as he slowly opened the package. Inside, he found a small Matchbox pickup truck and a key. He was speechless, realizing immediately what they had done. His newly rich granddaughter and her husband had bought him a real pickup, and it was probably outside. He'd never had one before, and he wept with joy.

Michele's gift from Steve was even more astounding. He gave her a brown teddy bear, and when she undid its zipper, she saw her real gift—a three-and-a-half-carat diamond ring. She didn't know it yet, but Steve had paid $43,000 for it. When the employee at the jeweler's shop in Charlotte had asked him for information to fill out the mandatory cash-reporting form, Steve had provided a phony name and a made-up social security number.

Shortly after Christmas, in early January 1998, Steve and Michele invited their friends for a night on the town. They even set up Kelly with a blind date, knowing she and her husband were having problems. Steve rented a limousine that shuttled the group to a Charlotte steak house. He tipped the limo driver hundreds of dollars, giving him a twenty each time he opened the door.

After dinner, they were driven to a nearby nightclub called Crickets in Gastonia. Kelly and her date were decidedly not hitting it off. One sign of this was that her date was dancing closely with Michele. This justifiably perturbed Steve, whose reaction caused a scene. The manager at Crickets asked them to leave, and on his way out, Steve told the manager, in a huff, that he was going to come back one day and buy the place.

This wasn't a pipe dream. It would've been Steve's biggest non-house purchase yet. The place was a dive with pool tables, a dance floor, and a bar, but Steve figured it might be the perfect way to launder money. He soon had a rough marketing plan. He would change its name to The Big House—as in prison—and the slogan would be, "If you're gonna do the time, do it right." He and Michele had visited a similar bar in upstate New York. He talked with the owner and came up with a tentative purchase price of $450,000.

><

Completely underneath Steve Chambers's radar, Jody and Jennifer Calloway managed a smooth getaway from North Carolina with their approximately $1.3 million in twice-stolen money. Jennifer had family in Colorado, so they decided to move there. As part of their plan, each would tell the boss at their job that the other one was being transferred, and they would write almost identical resignation letters.

Twenty-eight-year-old Jody was a U.S. Air Force veteran who had worked two years at Pattons Inc., an air-compressor company. His hourly wage was $11.45. "Although I have been afforded a great opportunity with such an innovative company," Jody wrote his boss, "I am putting my two-week notice in. My wife has accepted a job outside of North Carolina which would be to our family's advantage. I am sad that I have to leave when I am just becoming fully proficient at my job. However, I would like to thank you for giving me the chance to work with and become part of a winning team."

Jennifer, a General Electric employee, wrote her boss, "Although I have been afforded a great opportunity to work with such an innovative company, I am putting my two-week notice in. My husband has accepted a job outside of North Carolina which would be to our family's advantage. I am sad that I have to leave when I am just becoming fully proficient at my job. However, I would like to thank you for giving me the chance to become part of a world-winning team. I am very proud to say that I have worked for GE. Since I have worked here I actually felt myself grow as an individual and professionally. I hope that one day our paths will cross again.

"Again, thank you," she finished, "for the invaluable experience of what a company should be."

Her last day was January 9, 1998. They moved to Littleton, Colorado, where they used their stolen cash to persuade a landlord to rent them a house despite their lack of employment. They accomplished this by paying their security deposit and six months of rent up front. Their home in Littleton was nothing like Steve and Michele's mansion in North Carolina, but it was a significant upgrade from their Carolina living arrangements. It had 1,400 square feet, a finished basement, and a two-car garage. They bought two vehicles—a Ford Explorer for $32,784 and a year-old Chevy Tahoe for $23,982.

This was more money than they'd been able to spend before, but it didn't raise any eyebrows in Colorado, where they weren't previously well-known to the community. And unlike their unwitting North Carolina benefactors, who set off red flags everywhere they went, flashing their cash all over the place, the Calloways took out five-year loans, lived relatively quietly, and perhaps most importantly, had moved two time zones away from the scene of the crime.

A Careful David

He was lonely in Mexico with nowhere else to go. His wife probably loathed the very thought of him. His new honey in North Carolina was stalling him. And to make matters worse, the man making his cash drops was likely trying to kill him.

In January 1998, David Ghantt began to wish he'd never stolen the money. Though he still felt no remorse for what he'd done to Loomis Fargo, he increasingly wondered if the heist was worth it, since the stolen money seemed completely beyond his control and, more importantly, it wasn't clear how much longer he'd be alive. Occasionally—just occasionally—he thought of calling the FBI with the truth about the heist and the hit man.

His nerves had been shot ever since Robert told him that Bruno was working to kill him. Having been recognized as the Loomis thief at the Hard Rock Café had paled in comparison as a panic inducer.

He was now staying at hotels in Playa del Carmen. Its beaches lacked the beauty of Cancun's, but the odds seemed slimmer that he would be recognized. Still, he nervously looked over his shoulder as he walked the streets, wondering if Bruno was stalking him among the other pedestrians or maybe lying in wait somewhere with a rifle and a scope.

Two or three times a day when David walked the avenues, he cut through side alleys and turned his head to see if anybody was following him. If that didn't reveal anything—and it never did—he would stop suddenly, turn around, and smoke a cigarette for two minutes, just to see if anyone else had changed paths abruptly or looked as though they didn't fit in. While getting his hair dyed brown one day, he overheard other men in the barbershop use the word *policia*. He excused himself to go to the bathroom, left twenty dollars, and bolted out the back with his hair half-dyed. He washed out the brown dye once in his room.

At restaurants, he sat near the exit and the bathrooms, so that he was always ready to slip away if necessary. At night, he kept the lights on, staying awake partially out of fear and partially because the lights were on. Some nights, he stayed up with a pot of coffee; on others, he'd down an entire bottle of Jack Daniel's.

He didn't know that Bruno was actually Mike McKinney, but he stopped using McKinney's name for himself out of concern he would be traced. Instead, he used the name James Kelly, because it was similar to John Kelly, a character he enjoyed from Tom Clancy's novel *Without Remorse*. He went by the name John Clark, from the same novel, at the Hotel El Tukan in Playa del Carmen. He even checked into one motel under the name George Jetson, from the cartoon.

Just being in Cancun and Playa del Carmen, with their non-stop throngs of pleasure-seekers, was making him lonely and isolated. He began to miss his wife. Life with Tammy hadn't been terribly exciting, but it was safe and predictable, especially after they married in 1992 and moved to Hilton Head to live with David's sister. On weekends, they would walk along the beach and play Skee-Ball and video games at the arcade.

They had moved back to Gastonia three years later and lived with her parents for six months, but then they rented a place of their own. Every Friday night, they would go out to eat, either for fried fish, Chinese food, or steaks.

Tammy had loved him. He had loved her. He thought back to how they'd met at the Winn-Dixie, to how it ended the first time when she dumped him, to how their romance was slowly rekindled through the mail while he was in the Persian Gulf. He even had a fond memory of how she lost her diamond engagement ring—down the toilet, by accident—and just wore the wedding band. Did she still wear it? Did she still love him? He doubted he'd ever see or talk to her again.

He also wished he could find a way to let his parents know he was alive. He knew his mother was heartbroken and probably depressed. But he figured the FBI was watching his family closely. If he called Tammy or his parents, the authorities would trace the contact, and as bad as he felt, he didn't want to risk getting captured or getting them in trouble, which might happen if they hid contact with him from the FBI.

In addition, it never escaped David that his marriage and his life in North Carolina hadn't satisfied him when he was there.

He had absolutely despised working at Loomis Fargo, and he and Tammy didn't get to see each other as much as spouses should. And while she knew she wanted children, he wasn't sure fatherhood was for him.

≍

For most of January, David stayed inside his hotel rooms, watching HBO and eating M&M's. He watched a seemingly endless loop of *Men in Black*, with Will Smith and Tommy Lee Jones, and *GoldenEye*, the James Bond movie. There were times he would have gladly traded his depression and his loneliness at the holidays for the predictable life he had fled.

As for Bruno, David decided he would meet with him only in a public place. There'd be no more hotel or apartment meetings. Bruno resisted but realized he had no choice, so their next meeting was at a restaurant. Bruno didn't bring any money, telling David he had given it to Robert, who would pass it along to him.

So David arranged to see Robert, who again warned him not to meet Bruno anywhere that wasn't public. Robert also told David he'd decided not to meet with David anymore because the situation was becoming too risky, too dangerous. In late January 1998, when David and Bruno next spoke, David told him to leave the latest $10,000 cash drop with a third party. David would then retrieve it from that person. Bruno resisted, and in a case of the pot calling the kettle black, he accused David of trying to set him up. But David would have none of it.

"I don't give a damn about you. *Fuck* you," David said. And he hung up on Bruno, who realized Robert had probably blown his cover.

At least Bruno could now spend the $10,000 around town. He would tell Steve that airport police in Dallas had stopped him on his plane connection and taken it.

As for David, he remained at the mercy of his fellow thieves if he wanted his share. In mid-February, he told Kelly, on the phone, about his argument with Bruno. He said he was considering turning himself in.

Desperate to outwit any followers, he booked a room at a quiet inn, the Hotel La Tortuga. It was just a two-minute walk from Avenida 5 (Fifth Avenue), Playa del Carmen's popular pedestrian strip of bars, restaurants, and mariachi bands, but David stayed alone in his room most of the time, reserving it day by day under the name James T. Kelly and paying with wads of cash that he would remove, crumpled, from his pocket.

He would place the money on the front desk and say, "Take out what you need for another night." His ninety-dollar room was cooled by a ceiling fan and had a king-sized bed, a TV, and a whirlpool. Each day, the attendant had to restock his room's minibar supply of M&M's with two new packs. The hotel staff found him strange.

He never stopped talking with Kelly, persuading her in February to wire him $5,000. From a Western Union in Gastonia, she sent the money to a Michael McKinney. It would tide David over for a while.

Despite his stated concerns, Kelly kept telling David to meet with Bruno. He wondered if she knew about this supposed murder plot, though his suspicions weren't deep enough that he ever stopped wanting and asking her to come to Mexico. He told her he loved her, but she made no commitments, even when he tried to add to her worries about staying in North Carolina.

"I'll bet you money your phone's tapped right now," he told her. She may have cringed in fear, but she didn't budge.

⋇

Meanwhile, Tammy Ghantt was living with her parents nearly full-time, trying to keep sane by taking her young niece to the movies.

When David lived with her, they had spent different parts of Christmas at each other's parents' houses—Christmas Eve with her folks, Christmas Day with his. This year it was different. In mid-December, Tammy visited David's family in Hendersonville. It was a depressing scene, with conversation after conversation revolving around David, where he might be, and whether he was okay. They even talked to pictures of him, telling him to come home.

Sometimes, through the grief, Tammy managed a happy memory. She thought of David's goofy sense of humor. He could do great impersonations of the cartoon characters Ren and Stimpy, and of Tim Allen from *Home Improvement*. He would sing the Barney the Dinosaur song for kicks in a funny voice, and he would give his nieces and nephews "wet Willies," sticking his saliva-covered finger in their ears for a laugh.

He was a good husband, Tammy thought. Not a thief. He wouldn't have willingly deserted his wife, not in a million years. Somebody had to have put him up to it.

Coming Together

In early January, an intriguing piece of information crossed the desk of FBI agent John Wydra. Kelly Campbell's new minivan, according to his record checks, had been titled to herself and a man named Robert Dean Wilson. The second name sounded familiar to Wydra. It was an alias for Steven Eugene Chambers when he had scammed money from banks.

This seemed like the connection the FBI was looking for, appearing to tie Steve Chambers to Kelly Campbell, who agents had already comfortably tied to David Ghantt. But they needed to investigate further. They didn't know for sure the buyer wasn't a genuine Robert Wilson.

So Wydra and another agent drove to the Harrelson Toyota dealership in Fort Mill, South Carolina. Records showed the minivan was bought there, and they wanted to speak with the salesman who sold it. They showed him pictures of Campbell and Chambers and asked if they were the two who bought the vehicle. The salesman said yes, adding that the purchase had stood out to him because they had paid entirely in twenties, bringing the money on two separate occasions. The agents had already suspected an all-cash purchase, as the records made no mention of a loan.

On January 12, as agents considered their next step, the FBI received a visit from a man claiming to be an old friend of Steve Chambers. He was accompanied by a lawyer and his uncle, who was a private investigator. The lawyer had contacted the FBI two days earlier, so the FBI already knew the reason for the visit.

The friend told the agents he had known Steve Chambers a long time ago, had lost contact, and was now hanging out with him again. A few days earlier, Chambers had offered him $100,000 to take $2.5 million to the Cayman Islands. Wanting to do it, he had asked his uncle if anything seemed fishy or illegal about the deal, which of course it did. The uncle wasted no time calling his lawyer, after which they contacted the FBI. The agent who they spoke to told them Chambers was being watched by the bureau and persuaded them to bring the nephew in to speak with agents there.

The nephew said he had been suspicious about the source of Steve's wealth after seeing his new house in Cramer Mountain. He told them Steve had explained his riches with the line, "It all comes from taking risks." He also said Chambers had invited him to the New Year's Eve party at his house, and that Kelly Campbell was there.

Agent Rozzi told the nephew that the FBI was already investigating Chambers, Campbell, and Payne, but that they hadn't finished. Rozzi asked if he would consider helping them gather evidence by letting his phone conversations with Steve be taped. The FBI wanted to see if Steve would admit involvement in the heist or blurt out anything about David Ghantt. Rozzi explained that the FBI needed to find the stolen money and to locate Ghantt, who many agents believed was dead.

"We may have a murder on our hands," Rozzi said. "We've already heard what you've told us. But we haven't been able to get anybody inside this group."

The nephew was nervous. He had a family and a steady job, and becoming an informant would be stressful and take time. Rozzi told him the FBI would compensate him for any time he missed at work, if it came to that.

The nephew decided he would do it, and three months after the heist took place, the agents finally had someone in Steve Chambers's circle—an outer circle, perhaps—working for them.

When they had first heard about Steve Chambers in November among the dozens of confidential tips about possible suspects, the FBI agents figured he might be involved in drugs or gambling or securities fraud, or maybe a Ponzi scheme. He had a big house and big money, having made a major move despite lacking a legitimate source of income. But the newly discovered mini-van purchase erased all doubt from the minds of Wydra and the other agents about Steve's heist involvement. Still, they needed to be able to prove that involvement in court. And thus far they lacked evidence that the money Steve and Michele Chambers were spending around town came from Loomis Fargo.

On a mid-January afternoon, Wydra secured crucial proof. The minivan connection had spurred the FBI to increase physical surveillance of the Chamberses. And so on Friday, January 16, Wydra and David Sousa, an Internal Revenue Service investigator, were waiting at the First Gaston Bank in Mount Holly for Michele Chambers to come deposit money. She didn't disappoint them, keeping to her regular practice of making deposits on Mondays, Wednesdays, or Fridays, a schedule the FBI became aware of through bank records.

Wydra and Sousa were sitting in the branch manager's office when Michele walked inside, waited in line, and stepped up to the teller. She had $8,000 with her in a stack of bills with a thin white strip around it. Wydra and Sousa watched the teller take the money, remove the strip, and throw it in the trash can next to her station. When Michele left the bank, Wydra and Sousa immediately walked to the teller's station and looked in the trash can, which was empty except for the strip. Wydra picked it up and saw that it had signed initials on it.

He took it back to his office. Checking with Loomis officials, he learned that the initials belonged to a company employee who had counted money in the vault prior to October 4 but had been transferred to other duties afterward and had not since initialed wrappers around stacks of cash. That meant not only that Steve and Michele were using money from Loomis Fargo, but also that it had come from the company on October 4, since none had been reported missing from earlier dates.

This was a major turn in the investigation, and many agents now felt the case was essentially solved. But there was division in the bureau over when arrests should be made. Some agents felt the time was ripe. They now had their sights on a couple who obviously had Loomis Fargo money and were spending hundreds of thousands of dollars around town. But others worried that making arrests without knowing the locations of Ghantt and the rest of the money could backfire. After all, while they knew the Chamberses were involved, the agents couldn't assume they possessed all the stolen cash.

If the FBI arrested Chambers and Campbell while Ghantt or somebody else had the bulk of the money elsewhere, the bureau might never recover it. And if Ghantt were actually dead with no confession or body present to prove it, the defendants could simply lie and say he was on the run somewhere. And what if they'd planned to hide most of the cash and keep mum if some of them got arrested? In addition, the agents had no clear proof that Steve and Michele Chambers had actually helped Ghantt steal the Loomis money. Maybe other accomplices had passed it to them.

William Perry, who was in charge of the FBI's Charlotte office, decided the evidence accumulated to this point was too circumstantial to guarantee convictions. He wanted the agents to wait until they either found Ghantt and the money or could prove that Ghantt was dead. The agents started working seven-day weeks again, receiving help from FBI surveillance experts from New York and Atlanta.

As for Steve's old friend who agreed to let the FBI record him and Steve, the game plan was to have him goad Steve into talking about his involvement in the heist. The first few recorded calls, placed January 18 and January 20, failed to do that. Days later, doing what the FBI called "tickling the wires," he phoned Chambers and raised the issue to see how he would respond.

"I'm hearing stuff around town," he said, "that you had something to do with the Fargo heist."

Steve denied it. "That's just Eric running his mouth," he said, referring to Payne, who they both knew.

Steve seemed unlikely to implicate himself in the heist over the phone. But the FBI hoped he would at least allude to the aftermath. They wanted to listen to his phone conversations. While the tips and the house purchase pointed to him as the lead beneficiary and money manager, agents viewed wiretaps as the best way to find out what was really happening.

Obtaining judicial permission to install wiretaps was an involved process. In this decade before smartphones and texts would allow for new types of surveillance, eavesdropping on citizens' private phone conversations was as intrusive as law enforcement could be. Judges required—and still require—strong evidence from investigators that less intrusive methods had proven ineffective and that the wiretaps would help them solve a crime.

The supervisors called in agent Erik Blowers, an expert at securing judicial permission for electronic surveillance. The affidavit he prepared said that the bureau's investigative techniques thus far had proven insufficient and that wiretap authority would help secure the evidence needed to bring solid charges.

They had already tried physical surveillance, Blowers wrote, trying it on Campbell and Chambers, and while it had helped some, it ultimately wouldn't suffice because Chambers had previously worked as an FBI informant and was familiar with investigative techniques. Besides, he might be wary of surveillance, and performing serious undercover work was difficult in the gated Cramer Mountain community.

As for the use of confidential informants—also considered less intrusive than wiretaps—Blowers wrote that the ones they had were only on the fringes of the criminal operation and had been unable to provide the evidence they needed. And because of Steve's work as an informant, he might be wary of anybody showing increased interest in his activities.

Only wiretaps would get the FBI over the hump, Blowers wrote. From toll records and pen registers, agents knew that Chambers was talking to Kelly Campbell and Eric Payne, and the Chamberses' tax records showed incomes of less than $25,000 in each of the previous two years, barely enough to afford renting a single bedroom in the house they had just bought.

On February 10, U.S. district court judge Richard Voorhees approved wiretaps on the Chamberses' two home telephone lines. The standard wiretap rules applied—if a conversation was not related to criminal activity, the agents had to stop listening and recording, at least for a while. But as far as the investigation went, the FBI now had its most powerful tool yet.

Getting Close to Him

Steve Chambers loved mob movies and often used them as models for his behavior, but he ignored an important lesson from one of the best, *Goodfellas*: be careful what you say on the phone.

Henry Hill, a mobster played by Ray Liotta, laid it out: "Paulie hated phones," Liotta's character said, referring to New York crime boss Paulie Cicero. "He wouldn't have one in his house. He used to get all his calls secondhand. Then he'd have to call the people back from an outside phone."

That was so the FBI couldn't listen in. But four months after the heist, Steve figured the government still didn't know what he was up to. On his telephone, he talked about big purchases, about laundering money through the Gastonia nightclub he planned to buy, and even about hiring protection. With all this money around, he figured he needed a bodyguard.

✕

Even better, he could get two bodyguards. From his home, Steve called a personal security company on February 16 and asked the woman answering the phone about hiring two full-time bodyguards. He hung up without finalizing anything.

Full-time, professional bodyguards looked to be expensive, so Steve opted for a lesser degree of protection. On February 17, he called Mike McKinney, the hopeful hit man and former marine, and said he wanted to discuss a security arrangement for himself. McKinney accepted Steve's offer of a weekly $400 salary.

Security was not Steve's only concern. He needed to convert more of his cash to certified checks or money orders for the Crickets nightclub deal, which called for $250,000 in checks plus $200,000 in cash. That day, February 17, he spoke with his friend Mike Goodman, one of the people he'd paid to acquire checks for his house purchase. Steve told him he now wanted another certified check for $200,000, and that he would pay Goodman 20 percent, or $40,000, as a fee. Steve said he wanted a check just like last time—through the help of Goodman's wife, Kim, a bank teller. Kim told her husband to tell Steve that he and Michele should come to the bank when it wasn't busy, and that this time they shouldn't bring the cash in a briefcase.

Money aside, the Crickets purchase posed another problem that would be harder to resolve than by simply paying friends to convert cash to checks. The law forbade someone with a felony conviction to get a liquor license, and Steve had recently pleaded guilty to forty-two counts of obtaining property by false pretense. As things were, he wouldn't be able to get a liquor license. What he needed was to get his convictions pardoned.

His lawyer, Jeff Guller, said he knew an attorney who was known for working with government officials to help people get convictions pardoned. Steve said he was willing to pay this person $10,000 or $20,000 in up-front money, a sort of good-faith deposit, and that he ultimately would pay as much as $250,000 for a pardon.

><

In the midst of his domestic money laundering, Steve was still trying to have David Ghantt killed in Mexico or, failing that, to at least keep him satisfied to the extent that he wouldn't turn himself in and send the FBI their way.

On February 20, Kelly called Steve from a short vacation in Myrtle Beach. Without using David's name, she told Steve she had talked with him. She said he was growing nervous about McKinney, who David knew only as Bruno, and didn't want to deal with him anymore. They were going to have to send somebody else to make the next cash delivery, and it had to be soon, Kelly told Steve.

The next time David and Kelly talked, it would be to discuss his next move in Mexico. As far was Steve was concerned, this would be an important call. David would be giving them his new contact information. Steve wanted Kelly to call him with David's location as soon as she received it, so he could give it to McKinney.

At the appointed time, 7:00 p.m. on February 22, David called the pay phone outside a convenience store in Charlotte, where Kelly was supposed to be to pick it up. But Kelly had been too tired to drive from her Mount Holly home to take the call, so no one answered.

He called again at 7:17, and when a man standing nearby answered, David said he had the wrong number and hung up. At 7:29, when David called back, hoping against hope that Kelly would be there, the man picked up again.

"Who is it?" David asked.

"I'm just standing here, and I picked up the phone, man," the answerer said.

"Thank you very much," David said. And he hung up.

David wasn't the only person miffed at Kelly for missing the call. Steve was furious. He tried, in their next conversation, to impress on her the importance of getting David's new location.

Meanwhile, David paged her to arrange yet another call, this one for the next day. The pager message was 223984009898143—February 23, 1998, four o'clock, on phone number 9898 (the last four digits of the phone at the convenience store). Of course, the 143 meant "I love you."

This time, Kelly showed up for the call. David said he was near Cozumel, just off Mexico's Yucatan Peninsula.

"Coza-who?" Kelly asked.

"Cozumel," David said. "Cozumel."

Actually, David was lying. He was really in Playa del Carmen, which was just a ferry ride from Cozumel, but he didn't want to reveal his actual location. He still didn't want to deal with Bruno. Kelly assured him somebody would visit with more cash at 5:00 p.m. on either of the next two days.

David gave Kelly an answering-service number for the person making the delivery. Then he changed the subject, pressing her again to come to Mexico. This time, Kelly didn't even offer an excuse. She told him she wasn't certain anymore that life in a different country would suit her. She didn't say outright that she would never move down, but David was worried. Was she backing out of the plan? Something seemed off about her. She told him that while she used to think more money would make her happy, now she wasn't so sure.

Before they hung up, they expressed love for each other. Still, David was confused.

Kelly was not. She immediately called Steve with David's location and contact number, mentioning again that he didn't want to deal with McKinney. Details of the murder plot came up, and again they discussed injecting him with a fatal dose of bleach. Steve suggested that Kelly travel to Mexico to draw David out for the killer. Maybe she could make love to him, and somebody else could inject him with Clorox.

Whichever method of murder they would ultimately choose, David's reluctance to deal with McKinney presented a serious problem, and Steve knew it.

"He's absolutely saying he don't want you to come back down there," Steve told McKinney on the phone. "So the only thing I'm wondering is, how are you gonna get close to him?"

"It all depends where he's at," McKinney said. "Unless we send somebody—a decoy—down there, and I can shadow him."

The decoy idea sounded good to Steve. "You might need to call and cancel that reservation for in the morning and let [me] see if we can get somebody down there who can pull him out. That's the only damn thing I know to do, 'cause he'll see you coming from a mile away now… I don't guess there's a way you can get hold of a rifle or any damn thing?"

"I probably could," McKinney said. "But it'd take me forever to get it."

"If he won't take nothing from you, I don't know how else you can get close enough to him," Steve said. "You know what I'm saying?"

"Well, there's ways," McKinney said.

"I don't want you going in there and trying to do it and you not being able to do it," Steve said. "You know what I'm saying?"

"Yeah," McKinney said.

"That might fuck up the whole situation all the way around," Steve said. "Like I said, just hang tight until the morning, and I'll call… I'll know if we can get this person to pull him out and, you know, get close to him or whatever, and then that way give you a chance to get close to him and do it that way."

The decoy being discussed was Nathan Grant, Steve's cousin who had maintained his trust through the locker incident in Lincoln County that cost Steve about $1.3 million. Steve told his cousin he would pay him $1,000 to fly to Mexico to give someone twenty grand. For his plane ticket, Nathan would be using his middle name, Tommy.

On Sunday, March 1, Steve called Nathan to his house and gave him $24,000 in cash. He said Nathan should give half of it to his traveling partner the next morning. The plan was that when they arrived in Mexico, they should, between them, give $20,000 to the recipient. Nathan and his traveling partner could each keep $2,000 for themselves.

Taking Care of Business

Even in the midst of a murder plot, Steve's mind was on other things. He was wheeling and dealing on multiple fronts, or at least trying to. His efforts were involving him in activities everywhere from Gastonia to Raleigh to Mexico City.

In Gastonia, Mike Staley wanted more money than the $25,000 Steve had given him for his furniture store, and he was dropping hints he would make life difficult if he wasn't satisfied. Having been inside Steve's house and seen a bag filled with cash, he suspected Steve was involved in the Loomis Fargo heist. One day, after accusing Steve of stalling on the payments he expected, Staley looked straight at him and said, "I hope you burned your clothes." Steve stared back and said nothing.

At the moment, Steve didn't want to anger anybody who might pose a problem for him. He asked his lawyer, Jeff Guller, to prepare a promissory note saying he owed Staley $20,000 more.

"It's just more or less a little mumbo-jumbo shit between

us," Steve told Guller over the phone on February 24. "Staley knows he's going to be paid cash to him any damn way, so he ain't going to fuck around and say too much about nothing."

"Yeah," Guller said.

"Just every four months, the first of the month, he wants, you know, five grand."

"Okay," Guller said. He asked Steve what the money was for.

"It's just an agreement between me and him about something he's done for me, you know what I'm saying?"

"Okay."

"Something kind of under the table," Steve said.

"Gotcha," Guller said. "So I'll just put 'For services rendered.'"

The conversation then turned to the pardon Steve wanted that would help him buy the nightclub. Guller said he had pursued the matter and that it would take between six and eight months to get it, because Steve's convictions were only four months old. Also, the $10,000 or $20,000 required up front wouldn't buy total assurance that the pardon would come through.

"I have made the inquiries, and I have kind of stayed after them," Guller said. "I've gotten it going as far as I can get it going for right now without now starting to put some money toward it."

Steve had viewed the transaction as a sure thing. He didn't want to risk throwing money away. "I just don't want this shit stuffed in somebody's damn pocket," he said.

"No," Guller said. "Not at all. See, I'm getting involved with it to make sure things are going on."

Steve asked what it would cost him.

"You said, 'I'm willing to spend $250,000' on Friday," Guller said. "And certainly, I don't want it to cost that much… I want to keep it under $100,000 if I can, but you know, I don't know."

"Right," Steve said.

"I'm not even telling anybody you're willing to go that high," Guller said. "I want them to come back to me and say, 'Okay, we need ten here, ten there, and ten there.' Fine. But I'm not even willing to say you are willing to go to any more than that."

Steve asked Guller when he needed the first payment.

"Yesterday," Guller said. "Just whenever."

But before the pardon could be arranged, Steve decided to back out of the Crickets deal. Guller advised him that keeping the required alcohol records for the state would be burdensome. Steve had paid the nightclub owner $100,000 as a deposit but got it back, using the excuse that someone from the Internal Revenue Service was asking him about the deal.

Final Touches

David Ghantt was probably alive. To the FBI, that was the wire-taps' most important revelation.

The agents had done a lot of listening since Judge Voorhees let them secretly record Steve's phone calls beginning February 11. The first clue that Ghantt was alive came on February 20, when agents recorded a call between Steve Chambers and Kelly Campbell. While Ghantt wasn't mentioned by name, Campbell said she had talked to "him," and that "he" needed a new person to "make the drop" to him in the near future. She'd said his next call to her would be February 22 at 7:00 p.m. outside the Nichols Food Store in Charlotte. Chambers told her to find out how much money he wanted.

Other calls showed that Chambers was spending money like there was no tomorrow. They heard about the $43,000 diamond ring. Agents heard him consider buying a Rolex and hiring a bodyguard. They heard him discuss money laundering and buying the Crickets nightclub. But they never heard him say anything on the phone that unmistakably implicated him in the heist or indicated where the money was.

On February 21, they heard the suspects getting nervous. "People are talking," Eric Payne told Chambers over the phone, before suggesting that Chambers beat up whoever was saying they were involved in the heist.

Agents also listened to a recording that almost stopped their hearts. The Charlotte-Mecklenburg Police left a message on Steve's answering machine telling him there was a warrant for his arrest involving a worthless check—a check unrelated to the heist, of course. The police left a number to call. The agents acted fast, persuading a Charlotte police supervisor to hold off on pursuing the worthless-check charge, due to more pressing matters.

⋙⋘

While Campbell and Chambers seemed to be talking about David Ghantt, the FBI wanted to be certain. They received permission from a federal judge to wiretap the pay phones outside Nichols Food Store and were present at the call Ghantt made on February 22 when Campbell had not shown up.

To be on the safe side, the FBI had sent undercover agents to wait outside the store at both 7:00 a.m. and 7:00 p.m., when they believed the unnamed "he" was supposed to call there.

No one called that morning. In the evening, two agents with cameras sat in a car outside the store, ready to snap into the rearview mirror to catch an image of Campbell on the pay phone. Three other agents sat at a table inside the store. They all expected this to be a big break in the investigation, and when 7:00 p.m. came and went, they figured she was just running a little late.

She never arrived. At 7:17 p.m., a pay phone outside the store rang. The undercover agents stood by as phone surveillance machines monitored by their colleagues traced the call to somewhere in Mexico. Did that mean Ghantt was in Mexico? There was no way to know for sure, because when agent Brian Roepe picked up the phone and said hello, the man on the other end said, "I have the wrong number," and hung up.

The phone rang again at seventy twenty-three and stopped when no one answered. When it rang a third time at seven twenty-nine, Roepe picked it up.

"Who is it?" the caller asked.

"I'm just standing here, and I picked up the phone, man," Roepe said.

"Thank you very much," the caller said and hung up.

The consensus in the bureau was that it had to be Ghantt. The man had called when Ghantt's beeper transmission told them to expect a call. The agents' confidence was strengthened by a call recorded that evening between Chambers and Campbell. When Chambers asked if Campbell talked to their caller as expected, she said she had been too tired to drive to the pay phone. Exasperated, Chambers told her he needed to know where the caller was, so he could send his people "down there."

Later that evening, Campbell called Chambers back and told him another call would come through at 4:00 p.m. the next day. Chambers told her not to miss it and to call him after the conversation.

The next day, February 23, the FBI recorded the phone call between Campbell and a man agents now *knew* was David Ghantt. An undercover agent snapped a picture of Kelly talking on the phone outside the store. In the conversation, Ghantt said he was around Cozumel, Mexico, and gave Kelly a phone number for the money deliverer to call him once he arrived. Ghantt told Campbell he loved her, strengthening the agents' suspicion of a relationship between the two.

But her ensuing call to Chambers alarmed the FBI, as did other calls that agents heard on February 24 between Chambers and Mike McKinney, who discussed rifles, human decoys, and "getting close" to somebody. It was clear that Ghantt's coconspirators were talking about trying to kill him. Campbell was giving information to Chambers about Ghantt's whereabouts, and Chambers was using that information to plot his murder. The scheme appeared to involve cash deliveries, though it was unclear to the FBI why Chambers would give money to a man he was trying to kill.

Knowing about the murder plot changed everything for the investigation. Saving Ghantt's life now became the top priority. Agents had to find him and take him into custody before somebody killed him, even if blowing their cover meant recovering less cash.

But they had to figure out where he was first. While Ghantt had said he was in Cozumel, the FBI didn't know his exact location. The Mexican phone company hadn't been able to track his last call.

The agents even tried to insert their informant into the mix, telling Steve's old friend to try to persuade Chambers to send him to visit Ghantt in Mexico, rather than McKinney. The agents advised the friend to bad-mouth McKinney's reliability so Chambers would send the friend instead. A golf date with Chambers was scheduled where the informant planned to discuss this, but it rained, so they postponed it.

The bureau's supervisors wanted to send four agents to Mexico to find Ghantt. But first they needed clearance from the Mexican authorities, because the United States isn't supposed to send working law-enforcement officers abroad without permission from the host country.

The Mexicans' response to the request was not to the FBI's liking. The bureau was allowed to send just a single agent, and he had to be unarmed. This agent could accompany armed officers with Interpol, the international police agency that links police departments worldwide and that, in Mexico, was composed of select officers from Mexico City.

The bureau decided to send Mark Rozzi, one of the first agents to respond to the theft almost five months earlier. He left on a US Airways flight from Charlotte the next morning, and upon his arrival in Mexico City he met five Interpol officers who escorted him to a private police plane. It flew them to Cozumel, where they thought Ghantt was hiding.

The water and the beaches beckoned, but Rozzi had come to

work. He and the Mexican officers worked with phone-company officials to try to trace Ghantt's previous calls. Rozzi maintained that the calls should have come from a Cozumel number, because that's where Ghantt had said he was. But the company couldn't trace them.

As they waited for the phone company to come through, Rozzi and the officers tried the simplest approach possible— cold searches through Cozumel to find Ghantt. They split into two groups of three officers each and asked people if they had noticed a tall, thin, redheaded white man anywhere. The officers talked to drunk people and prostitutes, to bartenders and other local residents. More than a dozen people said they might know who he was, pointing to bars or hotels that they thought he frequented, but all the leads died.

Back in North Carolina, the agents continued recording and listening to calls. Chambers was continuing to relay information about Ghantt from Campbell to McKinney.

On February 25, upon learning that Chambers was supposed to visit McKinney the next morning at his room at the Hampton Inn in Gastonia, the FBI received permission to conduct microphone surveillance on the room. The agents listened to McKinney as he discussed making airline reservations to Mexico for himself and a man named Tommy Grant. Meanwhile, other agents heard Chambers tell Kelly Campbell, on the telephone, that "the guys" would be leaving the next morning and should arrive in Mexico around 6:30 p.m. Chambers then called McKinney to remind him to be on time at the airport Friday so he wouldn't miss the flight.

Then there was a glitch. Tommy Grant didn't have his traveling papers in order and needed some time. Chambers was angry. He called McKinney to delay the trip three days, until Monday, March 2, so Grant could get the certified copy of his birth certificate that he needed.

The FBI also intercepted an electronic message to Kelly's pager, apparently from Ghantt. The message contained the following number sequence: 227983009898143. Cross-matching that with phone numbers, the agents took the message to mean that on February 27, 1998, at three o'clock, Ghantt would call Campbell at the phone outside Nichols Food Store.

><

Agent Womble had an afternoon shift of manning the microphone in the hotel room next to McKinney's. He could tell that McKinney was there by himself. All Womble could hear through the wall was the sound of the suspect watching TV, downing booze, and then urinating for what seemed like forever. One time, McKinney kept it going for almost the length of two commercials. Womble realized he had had finer, more dignified moments as an investigator.

At 9:20 a.m. the next day, February 27, another agent was manning the microphone when Chambers arrived in McKinney's room. For the next thirty-eight minutes, the two talked about plans to murder Ghantt with a gun and how they would conceal it.

"If it fucks up," Chambers said, "we are all in a world of shit."

Glad to See You

Sure enough, Ghantt called Campbell at 3:00 p.m. on February 27. The agents heard him complain that nobody had arrived to give him money. Campbell, who had not yet heard from Chambers that the trip was delayed until March 2, said that someone would be in touch that day. Ghantt gave his phone number as 314-84, in room 101. Campbell said she would try to learn more details of the delivery for him, and Ghantt said he would call her back.

This time, Ghantt's call was traced quickly to the Hotel La Tortuga in Playa del Carmen. The agents finally knew exactly where he was.

They continued to monitor the phones, listening ten minutes later when Ghantt called Campbell again. They could sense his frustration when she had no new information for him. Their concern for his life didn't stop some agents from chuckling when Ghantt told Campbell he loved her and her response was, "I'm still gonna try to come down there."

※

Supervisor Rick Shaffer quickly contacted Rozzi with Ghantt's location, which Rozzi shared with his Interpol hosts. Two undercover Interpol officers—a man and a woman—checked into the Hotel La Tortuga pretending to be a married couple. After learning the hotel's layout, they told Rozzi he would stand out, thanks to his bushy American mustache. So he found a hotel elsewhere. Playa del Carmen was packed with tourists, and hotel rooms were hard to come by. Rozzi had to settle for a dump of an inn a few blocks away that had a power outage almost immediately after he checked in.

That day, February 27, the Interpol officers, using the FBI's pictures, identified Ghantt sitting at the hotel pool. They didn't arrest him on the spot, knowing they'd have to closely coordinate that with the FBI. In addition, they needed to ask Rozzi to confirm the man's identity. Rozzi walked into the hotel and saw his man in the lobby. It was Ghantt, all right.

In Charlotte, the FBI remained uncertain about exactly when the arrests should be made. Interpol officers continued tracking Ghantt as Rozzi waited for orders from North Carolina. Since McKinney's trip to Mexico was being delayed until March 2, there was less immediacy, and the FBI would use the extra time to continue searching for the stolen money.

The key to the whole operation, of course, was the Interpol officers' ability to keep track of Ghantt. To Rozzi's dismay, that was not a given.

Rozzi was stationed for hours at a time around the corner

from Ghantt's hotel. There, on the street, he waited to trail Ghantt's followers at a distance, in case they shadowed him leaving the place. On March 1, Rozzi saw the Interpol officers exiting the hotel with perplexed looks on their faces. They had lost him.

Rozzi's heart sank. But it turned out Ghantt was not running from them. He hadn't known they were there, and he returned to the hotel after some very nervous hours for the officers there. Once Ghantt was back in sight, Rozzi called the FBI in North Carolina and told Shaffer they needed to act fast because the Interpol officers obviously were not well trained in surveillance. If they didn't arrest Ghantt soon, they risked losing him.

"I can't promise you he's not going to get lost again, for good," Rozzi said.

Shaffer asked if they could wait a few hours. He also wanted Rozzi to see if his hosts would agree to not publicize anything about the arrest until the next day, March 2. That's when the bureau had decided to arrest Ghantt's cohorts in North Carolina, early that morning, shortly before McKinney and Tommy Grant were to fly to Mexico. If the news of Ghantt's arrest emerged too soon, the North Carolina suspects could get desperate. In the meantime, the FBI began lining up its own people and some local police officers so they could bring in all the suspects in North Carolina simultaneously.

Three hours later, as the sun was about to set on March 1, about five undercover Interpol officers approached David Scott Ghantt on a street near the Hotel La Tortuga. He was holding a laundry bag and apparently looking for a place to do a Sunday wash. Even before Ghantt noticed them, he seemed nervous, like he was scanning the streets for his killer.

One of the officers tapped him on the back and said, "Excuse me, sir."

Ghantt kept walking.

"Excuse me, sir," the officer said. "Could we see your passport?"

Ghantt stopped. As the officers surrounded him, he showed a picture identification with the name Michael McKinney.

The Interpol officer who had tapped him said, "You're not Mr. McKinney, are you, Mr. Ghantt?"

"No, I'm not," Ghantt said, turning his head and making eye contact for the first time with Rozzi, who was standing about five feet behind him. Ghantt seemed relieved to see an American in the crew. "Please," Ghantt said, staring at Rozzi, "tell me you're an FBI agent."

"Yes, I am," Rozzi said.

"I'm glad to see you," Ghantt said.

"I'm glad to see *you*, David," Rozzi said.

"You know, they wanted to kill me."

"I know," Rozzi said. "Don't talk about that now. We'll have a chance to talk."

All Over

With a handgun close by under a pillow, Steve Chambers was in a criminally rich man's slumber next to Michele when, just after 6:00 a.m. on March 2, there was a loud knock at the door.

Minutes earlier, outside his lovely house, about two dozen FBI agents and local police officers had adjusted their Kevlar bulletproof vests, rechecked their Sig Sauer, Glock, and Smith & Wesson handguns, and stealthily positioned themselves around his yard, away from the windows. Minutes before that, the agents and officers had driven a caravan of SUVs and cars up the winding road that led to 503 Stuart Ridge, passing through a neighborhood of luxury homes that the agents themselves could not afford. John Wydra, Rick Shaffer, and the other agents parked their cars a few homes away from that of Steve and Michele Chambers and silently prepared for what was next. As they approached their destination, they drew their guns.

Hearing the knocking, Steve arose from his bed, rubbed his

eyes, threw on a pair of boxers, and stumbled to the door. "Who is it?" he asked.

A man outside said he was a Gaston County police officer and that somebody had broken into Steve's furniture store. The police needed to talk to him.

Steve opened his door.

"FBI! Get down! Get down!" the agents yelled.

Steve dropped to the floor. "What the hell's going on?" he blurted out. Agents quickly surrounded him, handcuffed him, and placed him under arrest. He asked to speak to Phil King.

"Be careful," Shaffer advised the other agents preparing to occupy the home, room by room. "There are kids in the house."

Pointing their guns and flashlights, Wydra and Gerry Kidd, a Charlotte-Mecklenburg sheriff's deputy, rushed the bedroom, where Michele Chambers was huddled under the covers.

"Hands up!" Wydra and Kidd yelled together.

Michele obeyed, revealing that she was wearing nothing but her $43,000 diamond ring. Wydra still had his gun pointed at her. Michele, her hands in the air, realized her breasts were showing and moved to pull the covers around her.

"Hands back up!" Kidd shouted, worried she had a weapon in the bed.

Michele stood up, grabbed a bathrobe, and held it in front of her.

Wydra and the other agents were suspicious the robe contained a weapon. "Hands back up!" Wydra yelled.

For law-enforcement officers, a robe is a standard security check in a bedroom arrest. Wydra and the other male agents in the room turned away from Michele while a female agent checked the robe for weapons. It was clean, and Michele put it on. Then she removed her diamond ring at the agents' direction and placed it on the bathroom vanity. She would be allowed to dress and pack a bag for her children, she was told. The agents quickly discovered a handgun under a pillow on the bed.

While other agents began to take inventory of the couple's assets, Michele found the perfect moment when absolutely nobody's eyes but her own were on the diamond ring. She palmed it; after all, it was hers, she figured. When she walked into another room to pack a bag for her children, who would have to stay with her parents while she was in custody, it hit her that she was going to jail. She put the ring inside her children's suitcase. She also packed her Rolex and a diamond tennis bracelet.

She then called her parents' house. "I need you to come pick up the kids," she told her stepfather.

Dennis Floyd didn't understand why.

"Right now," Michele said. "Bye."

※

About the same time, five miles away in Gastonia, FBI agents poured into the Hampton Inn. From the front desk, one of them called room 403, inhabited by Michael McKinney. McKinney had fallen asleep only two and a half hours earlier. The book he was reading—*The Partner* by John Grisham, about a lawyer who fakes his own death and flees to Brazil with $90 million—was on his hotel night table. Groggy, he answered the telephone, figuring it was a wake-up call.

The voice on the phone asked if he was Mike McKinney.

He said he was.

The voice said the FBI was there and that he should open his door. McKinney did, and agents swarmed into his room.

Meanwhile, about five miles away in Mount Holly, agents called the mobile home of Kelly Campbell, who was still sleeping. The person on the phone told Kelly that it was the FBI, that she should open the door, and that she had better stay on the phone while doing so.

Kelly peeked through the window blinds. Police cars were everywhere. She grabbed a robe and opened the door. Agents rushed inside. A female agent made her drop the robe, checked it for weapons, and gave it back to her. An agent asked if she knew what this was about. "It's about the money stolen from Loomis Fargo," Kelly said. "That's the only thing the FBI has ever interviewed me about."

She put a shirt on and alerted the agents to her pistol on her nightstand. Annoyed by a female agent's glare, Kelly mouthed off: "What are you looking at?" The agent shrugged her off and they began looking through the home.

At the same time, twelve miles away in Belmont, agents knocked on the door of Eric Payne's mobile home. Eric yawned and walked to the door in his boxers. He figured it was a relative, though he had no idea who or why, since it was so early. He opened the door to FBI agents, who swarmed inside.

Eric told them he hadn't done anything. When agents soon

confronted him with $70,000 in bills just removed from his closet, he told them it was from gambling. They responded that he must be pretty good at it. Eric knew he was toast.

Early on, it was shaping up to be the worst day of their lives.

Steve and Michele had made the steepest ascent up the social ladder after the heist, and their fall back down had already begun. They were taken in separate FBI vehicles to the agency's Charlotte headquarters for interviews. When they hit Interstate 85, they were driving in the opposite direction on the same highway that the group had traveled with the stolen money the evening of the heist.

That October night and afterward, Steve had sworn his cohorts to keep their mouths shut if they were ever arrested. Now, five months later, knowing he probably faced the longest sentence of anyone involved, Steve decided right away to do what was best for Steve—namely, to tell the FBI about everyone. It's a paradox of criminal investigations with multiple defendants that the person facing the most serious charges often has the most to gain by confessing as soon as possible.

If Steve told the agents about everybody and promised to testify against them if they claimed innocence, he could expect leniency at sentencing. Those were the rules. People with less guilt generally have fewer such points to play. It isn't necessarily fair, but that's how the system works.

Steve had this in mind when, at about 8:00 a.m., he found

himself in an interview room at the FBI's offices in downtown Charlotte with agents Ray Duda and Bob Drdak, and with David Sousa of the IRS. The agents advised him of his Miranda rights, and Steve waived them, agreeing to be interviewed. Then he told them almost everything that popped into his mind about the previous five months.

It was Kelly Campbell, Steve said, who had approached him with the heist idea, saying she knew someone who worked at Loomis who might help them. He talked about getting Eric Payne and Scott Grant to assist, and of getting Mike McKinney to try and murder David Ghantt in Mexico. The most recent plan, he said, was for McKinney and Steve's cousin Nathan to fly to Mexico that very morning. Nathan knew nothing about the murder plot but would give Ghantt money while McKinney watched the delivery. McKinney would then trail Ghantt afterward.

Steve also told the feds about buying the BMW, Kelly's minivan, and Michele's $43,000 ring. He talked about getting the $200,000 cashier's check at First Union with the help of Mike and Kim Goodman. He mentioned his furniture store purchase and the possible nightclub deal. He talked about how he had paid Nathan Grant to keep the stolen money in storage facilities, until more than $1 million was stolen around Thanksgiving. The agents didn't know whether to believe him on that one, wondering if he had really hidden that money somewhere in case the law caught up with him.

Steve also named all the people he had paid to store money in safe-deposit boxes: Michele's parents, his own parents, Calvin Hodge, David Craig, and others. He said he never revealed the source of the money to any of these people but told them it came from bookmaking or gambling. The same information gap was true concerning his lawyer, Jeff Guller, who, he told the FBI, had managed his house purchase and received $10,000 to hold more than $400,000 of Steve's cash at his law office. Guller had also assisted him with other yet-to-be-completed transactions, Steve said.

None of these people had helped plan the heist. All had agreed to help Steve with various tasks—most of them for cash in return—and now, at his first opportunity, he was telling the FBI about their involvement.

><

In a separate room, Michele sat with agents John Wydra and Lucie VonderHaar. "I don't have anything to say," Michele said. "I'm not talking."

On a dry-erase board near her was an FBI chronology, in blue Magic Marker, of her and Steve's activities after the heist. She stuck to her guns.

Wydra played bad cop. After Michele's continued refusals to talk, Wydra stormed out of the interview room, quickly returned with a folder, and slammed it down on the table in front of her.

"You know what this is? These are pictures of you, Michele. I know you're involved in this."

Michele wouldn't admit to anything.

Wydra left the room again. When he came back moments later he had a VHS tape.

"We got you on videotape," he said. "Making bank deposits."

Michele resisted for several hours. Nothing worked on her.

"Michele, we know everything," Wydra said. "They're all in there. They're all talking. And they're all pointing the finger at you."

Michele still wouldn't confess to a single thing. After conferring, the agents decided to have Steve talk to her. They brought him in and left them alone. Steve was crying, the sight of which terrified Michele.

"I'm working it out," he told her. "Just tell them what you know."

At this moment, Michele realized she couldn't count on Steve's protection anymore. When he left, she began telling the agents about the house purchase and the furniture store, and revealed that she remembered counting more than $14 million at their home the night of the crime.

She told the agents she had not known, at first, that the money came from Loomis Fargo. When Wydra accused her of lying, she maintained she thought her husband had received it in return for holding money for "some friends up north." After the media coverage of the heist, she had started to wonder, but she preferred not to know for certain, so she never asked, she said.

In a different room, FBI agents Rick Schwein and Thomas Widman were interrogating Kelly Campbell. She too was obstinate at first, until they showed her a surveillance picture of herself talking on the phone at Nichols Food Store.

"Well, this is what happened," Kelly said. She told them about the plan, identifying Steve Chambers as the driving force. She said she had fed him information about David Ghantt's location in Mexico, and that there was a murder plot that Chambers and his supposed hit man obviously could not pull off. "Them SOBs have been going down since October and could not get close enough to kill him. *I* could've gone down there and done it myself," she said to the agents.

She said she knew Ghantt had a crush on her and that she had used his feelings to prod him to commit the theft, even paging him with 143 the day of the heist to encourage him. "How many chances do you get to talk someone into stealing $17 million for you?" she asked.

＞＜

In yet another room, Wydra and Dick Womble were meeting resistance from Eric Payne, who denied any involvement.

"Steve Chambers is ratting you out," Womble said. "Kelly's in another room, and she's ratting you out."

Eric didn't give in. He acknowledged knowing Steve but wouldn't admit to helping in the Loomis Fargo theft. He also said nothing about his wife's and sisters' breast implants.

"Just send him to jail," Wydra said to Womble.

"I'm already going to jail," Payne shot back.

In the back of their minds, or even up front, the people arrested had to have known this day might come. The same was probably true for the people who accepted money from Steve to hide or store his cash. Indeed, it wasn't just the thieves who were in trouble.

A warrant allowed the FBI to seize assets from the business trust account of attorney Jeff Guller. Agents Bart Boodee and Charlie Daly drove to Guller's office in Gastonia the morning of the arrests. The agents identified themselves and presented the seizure warrant. Guller invited them into his office.

They asked if he had done business with anybody listed on the warrant. He said yes, that he had done two real-estate deals with Steve Chambers—one for a $635,000 house and one for a $62,000 home in Lincoln County, and that the closing for the more expensive property had involved cashier's checks. When asked, he said he didn't know the source of Chambers's money for the closings. He said he had represented Chambers on worthless-check charges, that he had helped him with paperwork for his furniture store, and that he had conducted some legal work for Kelly Campbell, whose name also was on the warrant.

The agents let him know that Chambers and Campbell had been arrested in connection with the Loomis Fargo heist.

Public Defenders

At 11:00 a.m. that day, the FBI office in Charlotte hosted a packed press conference, with most of the questions fielded by U.S. Attorney Mark Calloway and William Perry of the FBI. They announced to the assembled media that they had found Ghantt in Playa del Carmen, and that he had been moving around Mexico since stealing the money five months earlier. They said he had benefited from significant help in North Carolina in planning and executing the crime, but that the FBI had already charged at least two of his cohorts with trying to kill him. Perry said the FBI had also obtained search warrants to look through the homes of various defendants in the Charlotte area, and that the reporters could obtain copies of a relevant affidavit at the federal courthouse.

For reporters, the forty-three-page affidavit was a gold mine. A quick glance made it obvious this story would be unforgettable. A $43,000 ring? A $635,000 house? A murder conspiracy? Breast implants? The details topped the TV news, both amazing and amusing almost everyone watching except for Sandra Floyd, Michele's mother, who saw the story while in the waiting room of Carolinas Medical Center, where her mother had just gone for tests. She heard her daughter's name mentioned and began to cry. She'd really believed the money came from gambling. The other people in the waiting room saw her crying and tried to comfort her, thinking somebody she knew had just died. As for the defendants themselves, most were scheduled to make their first court appearance at 2:00 p.m.

The FBI had seven people in custody. Most of them were led into Charlotte's imposing federal courthouse, the Charles R. Jonas Federal Building, for an appearance before Magistrate-Judge Carl Horn.

The hearing took place in a small courtroom with deep blue carpet, laid out with two and a half rows of benches that fit only twenty spectators. About ten more people could fit standing in the aisle. On this day, reporters packed the place, easily outnumbering the defendants' relatives.

The purpose of the initial hearing was to determine only whether the defendants, who sat one at a time at a polished wooden table just a few feet from the prosecutor's table, could afford their own lawyers or would need court-appointed ones.

"You're not employed and have no assets," Judge Horn said to Kelly Campbell while reviewing her paperwork. "You do have five thousand dollars in cash, is that right?"

Kelly, wearing blue-camouflage overalls, said the judge was correct but that her money had probably been confiscated.

She was right. FBI agents and federal marshals, armed with search warrants, were examining everything in the defendants' homes and seizing everything they thought had been bought with heist proceeds.

The most bizarre scene occurred at the Chambers home, where marshals were removing furniture, paintings, a grand piano, and other luxuries before a stunned audience of neighbors, who had no idea they lived so close to the heist's beneficiaries. The neighbors watched a steady stream from the house over the course of the day—the velvet Elvis, a Confederate throw blanket, a large oil painting of dogs in military clothes, the piano, two bronze statues of nude men, a white porcelain statue of three nude women, a sculpture of a headless man, a ceramic white elephant, a brass pineapple, gold-framed oil paintings of zebras, Dallas Cowboys team plaques, naked-woman bookends, a statue of a fat chef, and a trumpet. Through a first-floor window of the house, an agent could be seen feeding stacks of money into a bill-counting machine. Other agents removed guns found in the home—a Mossberg 12-gauge shotgun, a Beretta handgun, and an Interarms .38—along with fifty-four pieces of jewelry.

Two miles away at the furniture store, agents were seizing the inventory. Mike Staley came by and explained that he was owed about $50,000 on the business. But he lacked a written contract and knew almost immediately that he would see none of that money. He was right.

In the courtroom, Steve told Judge Horn that all he now

owned were eight acres and a double-wide trailer in Lincoln County, where his cousin Nathan Grant was living.

Without missing a beat, Horn turned to federal prosecutor David Keesler and asked, "Is there any intent to seize that property?"

Keesler said it was already seized. Horn looked back at Steve and joked, "You just became eligible for a court-appointed lawyer. Congratulations."

The courtroom crowd was still too shocked by and unfamiliar with the events unfolding to be amused by the irony of the rich man's need for a court-appointed attorney. The judge also kept Kelly, Steve and Michele, Eric Payne, Mike McKinney, and Nathan Grant in jail, assigning all of them court-appointed lawyers. Their bond hearings were scheduled for March 5, three days later.

On their way back to jail, the defendants walked outside the courthouse into a transfer van. Kelly and Michele were escorted separately from the male defendants. As news cameras stationed near the van clicked away, Kelly struck an unforgettable pose, waving at the photographers with her cuffed hands and acting as if it were time for a mock close-up. Behind her, Michele grinned. Photos of the goofy moment would be splattered across the next day's newspapers.

The eighth suspect arrested, Scott Grant, had peacefully turned himself in to FBI agents waiting at his home early in the afternoon. He had heard the news and figured they were looking for him. He drove to his mobile home, got out of his car, and said, "Here I am."

An agent asked, "Who are you?"

"Scott Grant."

"You're the man we're looking for."

Sixteen hundred miles west, this was a far less eventful day for Jody and Jennifer Calloway. More than three months after taking money from Steve's storage facility, the Calloways remained in Colorado. They had recently augmented their vehicle collection with a used Corvette and a Ford Mustang.

Their move stayed beneath the radar of the FBI and the defendants, most of whom did not know them. Jody was operating a small business called Rocky Mountain Woodworking with a man named Joseph Hamilton. Jody was the principal financier, giving his partner more than $50,000. He didn't tell him where it came from.

Flying Home

David Ghantt had a seat on US Airways flight 1514 from Cancun to Charlotte, which took off while his codefendants made their first court appearances. He ate a turkey sandwich. Mark Rozzi, who had paid Ghantt's bill at the Hotel La Tortuga on behalf of the FBI, sat next to him. As they soared above Florida in the early afternoon of March 2, 1998, Ghantt realized it was the first time he had been in the United States since the heist. He didn't know exactly what awaited him when he landed, other than prison. He thought his parents and Tammy would be initially thrilled to see him, though he wasn't sure how they'd feel afterward.

It was rare for a fugitive to be so happy being taken into custody. The evening of his arrest on the streets of Playa del Carmen, the cops had taken him back to the Hotel La Tortuga, where two of them had spent the night to keep an eye on him. He was neither surprised nor upset that they made him sleep handcuffed to the bed.

In the morning, as David was processed to leave the country, the Mexican authorities told him that because he had lived there with a fake ID—that of Mike McKinney—he was barred from returning to Mexico for one year. They had to be kidding, he thought. There was no way he'd be traveling *anywhere* for years to come.

David and Mark Rozzi had boarded the plane first and made their ways to the back row. David agreed to waive his Miranda rights, meaning Rozzi could interview him for the investigation. But before Rozzi started, his curiosity got the best of him. "What was up with you and Kelly Campbell?" he asked.

Ghantt looked down, and Rozzi noticed his eyes moisten. "I was in love with her," he said.

Still curious, Rozzi asked how far things had gone.

"I only kissed her," Ghantt said. "I only kissed her one time. Pretty expensive fuckin' kiss, wasn't it?"

Rozzi began his formal interview, almost whispering his questions so other passengers couldn't eavesdrop. Where had David stayed in Mexico? Whom had he talked to? How had he gotten involved in this in the first place? While writing Ghantt's answers down in a notebook, Rozzi noticed that flight attendants were watching them in amazement. News of the heist arrests had broken that morning, and some of them had heard about it while in Charlotte before flying to Cancun. Meanwhile, nearby passengers were suspending their own conversations to try to listen in and were quietly whispering things like "Holy shit! That's the guy!"

Ghantt told Rozzi how he had stolen the money, how he had

worked with Kelly Campbell to plan the heist, and how he had grown suspicious his accomplices were working to kill him.

Rozzi told him the FBI believed Kelly Campbell was involved in the murder plot, and that he had with him tapes of the recorded conversations, just in case David had decided not to cooperate. Rozzi offered to play some for him.

David wasn't in the mood. He stared at the floor, realizing now, without needing to hear the tapes, that he had been duped more than he previously suspected. He was anxious to tell Rozzi everything, anxious to make sure the FBI knew that in the scheme of things, he was somewhat of a victim here. After all, he had feared for his life only one day earlier.

And Rozzi was anxious to write down everything David said, to ask every possible question. He didn't know that back in North Carolina, the other defendants were rolling over like bowling pins.

Rozzi informed Ghantt that the FBI had contacted his relatives and that they might be waiting for his flight. When the plane landed at 5:00 p.m., Rozzi and Ghantt were the last to get off. The other passengers, reaching for their items in the overhead bins, couldn't help glancing again at David before leaving. When all the other passengers were off, the FBI's Rick Shaffer came to the plane door to escort David.

David looked around but couldn't find his relatives. On the ground, before David entered an FBI car, Rozzi introduced Agent Duda to him. "Nice to meet you, David," Duda said. "I gotta ask you one thing. What was going on between you and Kelly Campbell?"

At this point in the investigation, the question didn't matter much. If it seemed out of left field, well, the agents working the case had wondered about David's motivation for leaving his wife and had followed his conversations with Campbell, most notably the unreturned "I love you."

Ghantt looked stunned. He had stolen $17 million and almost been killed, and all they cared about was whether he'd had sex with Kelly Campbell? This was the first question of *two* agents? He asked Rozzi, "Is he joking? Are you guys kidding me?"

Actually, life could've been worse for David Ghantt. Despite stealing $17 million, he was charged only with bank larceny and money laundering. And though those crimes technically had a combined maximum sentence of thirty years, he likely would be imprisoned less than a decade if he pleaded guilty, as he lacked a prior record.

Ghantt had nothing to fear in jail; instead, he found himself treated like a minor celebrity, even a hero. He had taken the money and run, and his guts drew respect from the other inmates.

David's mother came to see him that first night in jail. He quickly saw that his mother still loved him, still supported him. Sue Ghantt didn't yell at her son for abandoning his family. "You're my son," she said. "I love you." She told him how close she and Tammy had grown through the previous five months.

David told his mom that he assumed Tammy hated him now.

Sue Ghantt told him to call her, and he did that evening. This was the first time David and Tammy had spoken to each other in five months, and not unexpectedly the conversation was tense. She had been expecting the call, having talked to Sue. David told her that while he was scared to talk to her, he still cared about her and loved her. She still loved him too, though she wasn't feeling great about him at the moment.

"I thought I'd never see you again," she said.

"I thought I'd never see *you* again either," he said.

Her first questions were simple. Why did he do this to her? And if he still loved her, why didn't he call while he was away?

He explained that he wanted to protect her, that he didn't want to get her involved, that he figured the FBI would consider her an accessory if they talked. She seemed to believe this. But then she asked about the other woman. Tammy had heard in the news about his so-called relationship with Kelly Campbell.

She was just a friend, David said. Not much more.

Tammy asked him if he had sex with her.

"No," David said. "And that's the truth."

That made her feel much better, at least for now. Still, after they hung up, she began to cry.

The M&M's Contest

The federal courthouse had already closed when David Ghantt's plane landed late in the afternoon of March 2, the day everyone else was arrested, so his first court appearance was the following morning. Wearing an orange jail uniform, he walked into Magistrate-Judge Carl Horn's courtroom. Seeing Tammy, his parents, and his sisters there, he stared at them on his way to the defendant's table. His eyes brushed over Tammy. It was the first time he had seen her face in five months. She was in the first row, and she seemed glad he was alive, but she also looked stunned and hurt.

David told Judge Horn that he had no cash and was assigned a court-appointed lawyer.

As he walked out of the courtroom, David stared a few seconds at his family and whispered to his mother and sister, "I love you." Then he stared at Tammy. She stared back. No words were spoken.

That morning's main headline in the *Charlotte Observer* read simply, "Eight Jailed in Huge Heist." Another front-page headline asked, "Is This the Gang That Couldn't Think Straight?" over an article by columnist Tommy Tomlinson that read, in part, "There is no polite way to say this: These folks are not exactly the brightest bulbs in the chandelier," having indulged so soon after the theft in "five months of high rolling that would make Richie Rich blush."

An *Observer* reporter named Joe DePriest, dispatched by his editor to Ghantt's temporary home in Playa del Carmen, the Hotel La Tortuga, provided fodder for weeks of amusement back home with an article about Ghantt's life on the run.

"He was a peculiar *norteamericano* in a Caribbean town known for its oddballs," the story began, before quoting a hotel staff member who said Ghantt spent most of his time there alone in his room eating M&M's, listening to the Eagles, smoking Marlboro Lights, and reading comic books. If he went out, she said, it was to Burger King for meals and a nearby bar, Capitan Tutix, for tequila. Sometimes he just sat by the hotel pool, which was next to his room.

More than any other single piece of original reporting on the heist, this story set the tone for what followed. Here was a man who, it appeared, had stolen $17 million yet wanted nothing more out of life than candy, cigarettes, cheap liquor, and the Eagles for background music. A Charlotte radio station, WLNK, announced a call-in contest for a weeklong trip to Playa del Carmen. The winner would stay at the Hotel La Tortuga and receive the following: a supply of M&M's, Eagles CDs, comic books, $1,000 in a phony bank wrapper, and a Wonderbra, in honor of the heist-financed breast implants, which had been mentioned in the affidavit.

On another radio program, the *John Boy & Billy Big Show*, a recurring character named Marvin Webster drew laughs with this take on the news: "The dude that actually stole the money, he's down in some crappy hotel room with a big stack of comic books, a copy of *Hotel California*, and he's living off M&M's in the minibar, layin' low, waiting for the high sign. Meanwhile, his friends back home are running around like the Home Shopping Club on crack! Did you see some of the stuff they bought? Chevy Tahoe, BMW Z3, bunch of motorcycles.

"Yeah, no way this could've attracted any attention. They bought two or three computers, a $10,000 pool table, a $40,000 diamond ring. One guy bought his wife some new boobs… These dudes pull the crime of the century [and] would've gotten away with it except they couldn't walk into the 7-Eleven without buying $1,500 worth of beef jerky!"

Legal Trouble

Across the Charlotte region, the defendants' Gaston County roots added to the story's appeal. Among the few people named in court documents who didn't seem to fit the stereotype was Jeff Guller. Though he hadn't been charged with anything, his name was conspicuously included in the main affidavit that was made public the previous day, and the FBI had visited his office the day of the arrests.

In fact, at Guller's request, agents returned to his office the following day to discuss keeping his trust fund unfrozen so he could use it for a transaction involving another client. The agents had been briefed on what Steve Chambers had told the FBI about having kept cash in Guller's office for several weeks. If that was true, Guller himself could face criminal charges, and that type of case didn't come around very often.

In fact, no lawyer had ever been indicted on a federal money-laundering charge in that part of North Carolina. And Guller had a much more pedigreed background than the people who'd been arrested at this point, none of whom had ever been to a four-year college, let alone law school.

At his office, Guller was asked by the agents if Steve Chambers had ever brought him a large stash of money. Yes, Guller told them, Steve had brought over a black suitcase full of cash before the house closing and unzipped it to show what was inside. He had spoken with Guller about using it for the closing, but Guller said doing so would necessitate him signing a form indicating its source. Steve didn't want to do that, so they agreed that instead he would get cashier's checks for the required amount. Steve then took the suitcase and left his office, Guller said.

Chambers, of course, had told the FBI that he actually left the money with Guller, so Agent Bart Boodee pressed him. "Mr. Guller, was there any time when the suitcase or any other large amount of money was left with you in your office?"

Guller said, "There might've been a time during that conversation when Chambers got up and left and went out to his car for ten minutes or so, and while he was out at his car, the suitcase was with me alone here in the office." But Steve soon returned to the office, retrieved the suitcase, and left, Guller said.

Boodee pressed him again. "Are you certain there was not a time in your dealings with Mr. Chambers that Mr. Chambers left money in your office?"

"No," Guller said. "Absolutely not. Never, ever on any occasion would I have done that."

"This is an important issue we're talking about," Boodee said. "It's serious. It's a felony to lie or intentionally provide false

194

or fictitious information to an FBI agent… We can reexamine what you've said if you want to revisit it with me."

Guller sat quietly and then revised his story. He had not actually seen the contents of the suitcase when Steve brought it over, he said, and Steve had indeed left the cash at his office for about two weeks, before Guller eventually returned it after having removed $10,000 for himself. He said Steve had insisted he take the money, first as payment for storing the bag and then, after Guller repeatedly declined, as a Christmas gift.

Guller also told the agents about two deals that Steve had discussed that were never consummated. He said Steve had asked him if it was possible to buy land for Kelly's husband under a phony name, and that he replied it was not.

Boodee had brought a tape recorder and some cassettes to Guller's office. After Guller answered him, Boodee fast-forwarded a cassette with a wiretapped conversation in which Guller told Steve that it was indeed possible to put property in a fictitious name. It was clear the FBI was considering charging Guller with a crime.

Guller admitted to Boodee that the tape made him sound bad. "I was bullshitting my client to make him feel good," he said, adding that he eventually would have told Steve it was illegal. He admitted he had probably exercised bad judgment. "I should not have told him I was going to do it under an assumed name."

Boodee then asked about the conversation—recorded, of course—in which Guller and Steve discussed paying up to $250,000 to get Steve a pardon for his felony convictions. Guller said he hadn't meant any of it, and that he never intended to participate in a bribe.

Staying in Jail

On March 5, one after another, the main players in the case appeared before Judge Carl Horn at a bond hearing, hoping to be freed from jail until their trials.

All the defendants had well-respected court-appointed lawyers. The first one to argue before Judge Horn was Noell Tin, the attorney for David Ghantt. Tin's goal, and that of all the attorneys, was to persuade the judge that his client would not flee or do anything illegal while free before trial—in short, that his client had reasons to stick around that outweighed the incentive to leave town. Noting Ghantt's family ties, Tin called David's mother, Sue Ghantt, to testify on his behalf.

"I just want you to know," David's mother told the judge, "we have a very fine son. He's always been honest and trustworthy and dependable [and] loving and kind. He has not ever been violent."

It was heartbreaking to watch. David's mother, in her fifties with curly, graying hair and glasses, was a woman who loved her son unconditionally, who knew deep down that he had a good heart and wouldn't hurt a fly.

"It appears he may have made a mistake," she continued, "but we love him, and we support him, and we care for him. And I don't think you would regret letting him out in our care. We would appreciate it very much."

Tin told the judge that Ghantt, if freed on bond, could live with a relative in Gastonia or with his parents in Hendersonville. "There is only one other thing I can say to Your Honor, which is that my client is presumed innocent. There is a temptation to presume we know exactly what happened at this point, [but] the statutory and constitutional law is simple. He is treated simply as a man who is presumed innocent. He's never been arrested in his life. And those kinds of people ordinarily get bond in federal court. And sometimes, someone goes out of the country for reasons other than flight from law enforcement."

The prosecutor saw things differently. First of all, said Assistant U.S. Attorney David Keesler, between $6.6 million and $8 million remained missing. Ghantt might know its location and, if freed, run away with it. He already had abused a position of trust at Loomis Fargo, using his access to money to commit the crime, Keesler reminded the judge.

"I mention this because this is a case about greed," Keesler said, "and it's a case about what some people will do for money. None of these defendants ought to be allowed out when that sort of money is still out there, and we don't know where it is."

The weight of the evidence was overwhelming, Keesler said.

"Mr. Ghantt is on videotape removing money from the Loomis facility. Seventeen-plus million dollars of money."

Judge Horn, to no one's surprise, decided to keep Ghantt locked up, noting he would have a better chance at bail if the missing money was found.

When it was Kelly Campbell's turn, Horn started by mentioning the evidence that showed she helped mastermind the heist, that she smoked lots of marijuana, and that she knew about the murder plot. Ghantt, sitting next to her in the courtroom, stared at her with pain in his eyes, shaking his head.

Keesler stood up. "She was the link," he said, "between David Scott Ghantt, who was then employed at Loomis, and Mr. Chambers and the rest of these folks." She helped Ghantt get his phony ID to leave the country, and she had admitted her role to the FBI, Keesler said.

When Kelly's lawyer, James Gronquist, asked her family to stand, three rows of people—her pastor; her parents; her husband, Jimmy; and her two children—complied.

Her mother, Colleen Elmore, testified on her behalf, saying that Kelly, if freed, could live with her and work for her brother's construction business until her trial. "I know this is bad, and my daughter has to pay for what she's done, but I'm just asking you to let her go home until she goes to trial and be with her kids, because they may not see her until they're half-grown. I promise you I will handcuff her to my wrist if I have to, to see that she don't go nowhere. It's not right for them li'l young'uns not to get to be with their mama."

Judge Horn kept Kelly in jail, though he seemed sympathetic.

"This is a very sad situation," he said, "when you have children and families hurt by very poor choices that other family members make. I have never seen a defendant who, once they've been caught, doesn't wish that they had made a different choice earlier."

While the judge reviewed Eric Payne's paperwork, prosecutors noted he was part of the heist itself and was later caught on a wiretap talking about trying to intimidate Steve's old friend, who Payne thought was spreading rumors about their involvement in the heist.

Payne's lawyer, Chris Connelly, said his client was not a risk to flee and should be released from jail until his trial. "If he wanted to flee, he could have fled a long time ago and possibly not been apprehended," Connelly said. "But he stayed right here where he was, worked the same job, lived with his family, tried to get a better job, tried to pay off his trailer, tried to buy the land underneath it."

Judge Horn kept him in jail.

The next-to-last defendant up for bond was Michele Chambers. Whisler called her one of the prime beneficiaries of the heist, mentioning her trip to a bank and asking how much she could deposit without the bank having to file paperwork.

Her lawyer, Andy Culler, acknowledged her spending habits of the last five months but argued to Judge Horn that, in the scheme of things, Michele was just "a young woman who is doing what she is told, rather than necessarily planning and directing activities."

Michele's mother took the stand. Sandra Floyd told the judge that Michele had struggled before she met Steve Chambers because her first husband didn't pay enough to support their children. She said Michele could stay at her house if freed.

Keesler was geared to pounce. He asked Sandra Floyd if she was surprised that Michele and Steve could buy their furniture store and their big house a few months back.

"I was never really told exactly where or how they made their money," Sandra Floyd said, adding that Michele had told her it came from gambling.

Judge Horn asked her, "Did your daughter show you her forty-three-thousand-dollar ring?"

"I saw several rings she wore," Floyd said.

"Did they look like they were worth a hundred thousand dollars to you?"

"Yes."

"Did you think that that came from gambling earnings? Financing?"

"I know that they were a gift from her husband for Christmas."

Horn kept Michele in jail.

As they left the courtroom in shackles, heading back to jail, Ghantt and Kelly found themselves standing next to each other in a courthouse tunnel. David just looked at her.

"I'm sorry," Kelly said. "It wasn't me. It was Steve."

"Yeah, right," David said. He turned away, avoiding all eye contact as they walked toward the van that returned them to their cells.

Steve tried to sell him a different story. While his own bond hearing wasn't until the following week, he approached David in jail and blamed Kelly for the murder plot. "When she got that money, she just went nuts," he said.

David said nothing. He looked away and turned toward several non-heist inmates, who he saw were staring at them in amazement.

David's relationship with Tammy had warmed since his first day back. Now, he was talking with her every night from jail. He felt she was there for him, and Tammy felt like a wife again. The tension in their phone calls had slowly eased, and it seemed that Tammy still wanted to make their marriage work.

Inmates were not allowed to accept incoming calls, so David phoned her collect at night, making her laugh by identifying himself to the operator as "M&M's"—he had heard about the radio contest—or Rascals, their cat.

Tammy sent him a picture of her and beamed when he said he put it on the mirror in his cell to "pretty up the place." He said he had really missed her on Valentine's Day, while he was alone in Mexico. He told her that he didn't deserve her, that he knew the uncertainty had traumatized her.

But she was still angry at him. He had completely abandoned her to pursue a wild dream, and if it had succeeded, she'd have never heard from him again. The only way she could make sense of it was by rationalizing that this had been needed to help them improve what had apparently bothered him about their marriage. She still treasured her old, pre-heist memories of him and kept the key to their mobile home, which had been foreclosed on three months earlier when she couldn't make the payments.

They talked about what they would do when he left prison—probably sometime around 2006 or 2007, he figured. Maybe she would open a tanning salon. He would open a tree-trimming service, maybe a towing company. And they would go live somewhere else, probably in a different state, somewhere where people had never heard the name David Scott Ghantt.

Of Brain Size and Bust Size

The investigation wasn't over. In the hours and days after the arrests, federal agents drove around Gaston and Lincoln Counties, west of Charlotte, to banks and storage facilities and the defendants' homes, looking for stolen cash and the vehicles, jewelry, and electronics that had been bought with other heist proceeds. These searches bore fruit, often in the form of six-figure sums of cash.

Hours after they arrested Steve and Michele Chambers on March 2, agents found $565,602 in a cardboard box in an office desk drawer at 503 Stuart Ridge. In the same room, in a plastic bag, they found keys for safe-deposit boxes in banks across the area. The next day, they found $897,000 inside one safe-deposit box and $470,000 in another. Two days later, they found $360,000 in a box that was cosigned by Steve Chambers and David Craig, and $454,000 in a box that was cosigned by Calvin Hodge and Michele Chambers. Also that week, in a facility rented by Steve

Chambers and Calvin Hodge, agents located a blue barrel containing dry dog food over a piece of cloth. Underneath the cloth was $770,000.

More large sums were found in other safe-deposit boxes, the signatories being Steve, his aliases, and other friends and relatives.

In total, that week, agents located $9.8 million. Combined with the $3.3 million found in the Loomis van on October 6, 1997, two days after the heist, they now had recovered $12.9 million from the $17 million that was originally stolen. Brian Whisler, the assistant U.S. attorney at Steve's bond hearing on March 10, told Judge Horn that about $4.15 million remained missing, and that Steve shouldn't be released until it was found.

Chris Fialko, the court-appointed lawyer for Steve, didn't even bother to argue his client's case. In fact, he'd tried to cancel the hearing, knowing from the results of previous proceedings that his client's odds of success were almost nil, and that Horn would deny bond. He was right. Steve was led back to jail.

Steve's friends and relatives who opened and cosigned for access to the safe-deposit boxes that held his money were now firmly within the FBI's cross hairs. On March 12, a grand jury returned a forty-nine-count indictment setting formal charges not only against the eight current defendants but also against nine other people, all of them relatives or friends of the first eight.

The new set of defendants included Michele's parents, Steve's parents, Nathan Grant's fiancée, Eric Payne's wife, David Craig,

Calvin Hodge, and Calvin Hodge's father. All were charged with money laundering for helping to hide the money. Each was freed on bond.

Among themselves, the prosecutors debated whether money-laundering charges, which had a twenty-year maximum sentence, were appropriate. Traditionally, money-laundering crimes involve schemes to turn stolen "dirty" money into "clean" money by running it through a seemingly legitimate business. But federal courts allow prosecutors to file a money-laundering charge when a specific act—for example, obtaining safe-deposit boxes in banks to hide dirty money—was performed with money that the defendant knew, or should have known, was illegally obtained. The crimes in question could seem more like concealment of stolen property than money laundering. But the harsher penalty for money laundering allowed prosecutors to pressure defendants to plead guilty.

None of these "money-stuffers," as the FBI called the defendants who hid cash for Steve in safe-deposit boxes, had been involved in the heist itself, and Steve apparently hadn't told any of them the money came from Loomis Fargo. Sandra and Dennis Floyd, for example, thought they were stowing Steve's gambling winnings. They had received $40,000 from Steve and Michele and used $13,000 of it for a pickup truck and $3,000 for a one-carat diamond ring.

The nine new defendants may have been shocked by their arrests, but at least they were free until their next court hearings.

Meanwhile, all original eight defendants remained behind bars through March 20, when Nathan Grant formally pleaded guilty and was released on bond until his sentencing hearing. Nathan entered a guilty plea to one count of money laundering, implicating himself in the storage of $400,000 in a safe-deposit box.

Prosecutors had more on him—for example, they knew Steve Chambers had paid him $70,000 to stash money just after the heist—but they agreed not to press other charges as part of the deal. His fiancée, Amy Grigg, charged the prior week with money laundering, sat in the first row of the courtroom watching the father of her child virtually ensure himself a prison sentence.

Nathan, a twenty-one-year-old mill worker, wouldn't know his fate right away. In federal court, sentences are usually imposed a few months after conviction. The judge freed him on bond, deeming him a safe bet to return to court for sentencing. He didn't return to the mobile home where Steve had let him live after the heist; federal marshals had seized that. Nathan moved in with his mother. Days later, after his brother Scott pleaded guilty to bank larceny and money laundering, the judge freed him on bond too, letting him live with their mother as well, as long as they agreed not to talk with each other about the crime.

Scott's involvement was viewed as more severe than his brother's. Unlike Nathan, he had been part of the theft itself. Nathan, on the other hand, had received more stolen money. Steve Chambers told agents he had promised Scott $200,000 for his role, but Scott had received only about $26,000, in increments of $6,000 or $7,000.

"He's remorseful about what transpired," Scott's lawyer, Keith Stroud, told the assembled press after the court hearing. "He wants to make the best of a bad situation."

Near the end of the month, on March 30, three key defendants were allowed to leave jail. Kelly Campbell, Michele Chambers, and Eric Payne had appealed the original denials of bond, and now all could go home to spend quality time with their families before their sentencing dates. They would have to wear ankle bracelets that would electronically alert authorities if they left their homes except for work and church.

The prosecutor, David Keesler, had opposed their release, while acknowledging in court that more of the missing money had been found—a total of $14.4 million in all, meaning $2.6 million remained unaccounted for. But he maintained that the three might know the location of that missing cash and try to flee with it. He described what they had done, noting that Kelly, for example, had helped plan the heist and participated in the murder plot. He mentioned that Michele helped rent the van used to move the stolen money and later used some of the cash to buy her breast implants.

Michele's lawyer, Andy Culler, objected, sensing an opportunity to set the record straight. Michele's breasts had become a laughing matter in media accounts of the heist arrests, because the FBI had thought she used heist proceeds to purchase her implants, information that made its way into an affidavit viewed by reporters. Culler, the lawyer, told the judge that Michele had actually bought her implants before the heist.

Michele herself clarified the matter further a week later, when an *Observer* reporter named Chip Wilson trekked to her parents' house to interview her.

"I do want to go on record to say I didn't get breast implants with this money," she told him, adding that she had paid for them in December 1996, ten months before the heist, and that she considered them a luxury. "It was something that I wanted to get," she said. "It increased my bust size, but it didn't decrease my brain size."

David Ghantt's lawyer thought that if Kelly Campbell was allowed out of jail on bond, David should be freed on bond as well. After all, Campbell had plotted to kill him, a more violent charge than anything Ghantt himself faced.

But on April 22, 1998, Judge Graham Mullen decided— reluctantly, he said—to keep Ghantt and Steve Chambers locked up. "I can't get around the notion that this is a fellow that stayed gone for five months," Mullen said. He added that he would also deny bond to Chambers, who, facing the most serious charges of anyone in the case, "clearly has the strongest motive of any of these defendants to flee." The government simply didn't believe Chambers's contention that much of the missing $2.6 million had been stolen from him.

Trials were scheduled for October 1998, but most observers thought that few, if any, would be necessary. There was strong evidence against almost everyone arrested. On April 24, Calvin Hodge pleaded guilty to money laundering, becoming the third defendant in the case to enter a guilty plea.

><

Meanwhile, as the weeks passed, it became increasingly clear to the bureau that they had a strong case against Jeffrey Guller and some other people named in the main affidavit that was made public after the arrests.

Guller knew that he might be in trouble, but he also knew that too much cooperation with the FBI could facilitate federal charges against him, and that he could lose his license to practice law.

His steadfast denials of wrongdoing only made the agents more determined. On June 2, a new indictment, charging Jeffrey Guller with money laundering, was made public. The most damning charge stated that he accepted a "bagful of currency" at his law office from Steve Chambers, stored it there at Steve's request, and took $10,000 for himself as a fee before returning it.

In court on the day of his arrest, Guller sat silently as his lawyer, Calvin Murphy, entered a not-guilty plea. Also in the courtroom were Kim and Michael Goodman, whose roles in helping the Chamberses convert $200,000 into a cashier's check had led to new money-laundering charges against them.

A week later, on June 9, Eric Payne became the fourth defendant to plead guilty. He told the court he had no idea what he was getting into when he decided to help Steve Chambers. "I'd like to say I'm sorry to the government and my family and my children that I've hurt through this," he said. "I'd like to put this all behind me and go on with my life."

Like Payne, Michele Chambers had been free on bail since early April. She had taken a job waitressing at a Chili's in Gastonia, where, despite all the recent publicity, few people recognized her, which suited her just fine. It also suited her that the FBI had not found the diamond ring, the Rolex, and the diamond tennis bracelet she had brazenly swiped just after she was arrested. She had since sold the Rolex to pay bills.

On August 3, she and Steve met in court for the first time since the arrests, becoming the next two people in the case to plead guilty. They sat next to each other at the defendants' table, him in an orange jail uniform and her in a sleeveless magenta dress. They whispered to each other several times and swore to tell the truth on the same Bible.

Michele's case was heard first. After she pleaded guilty to bank larceny and money laundering, the government dropped a charge of accessory after the fact. When it was her turn to address the court, she couldn't read the statement she prepared through her tears, so her lawyer read it on her behalf: "First, I'd like to say that I know what happened was wrong and I accept responsibility for my actions, but I'd also like to say that all of the people that are involved need to admit that Steve and I didn't do this thing alone. I am hoping that through my cooperation with this court and its affiliates, I can help to make certain that the truth finally does come out."

She also apologized to Loomis Fargo, its insurance company,

her children, the other defendants' children, and the friends and families of the people involved. She thanked God and her family for supporting her and professed her love for Steve: "I want to just tell you I love you and I'll be here for you. Thank you for loving me through all of the bad times in my life. You've always been here for me and helped me to be strong, and I know that one day God will bring us back together."

Steve, who looked like he had lost fifty pounds since his arrest, probably because of the food in jail, was less verbal and answered quietly when the judge talked to him. He pleaded guilty to bank larceny, accessory to bank larceny, conspiracy to murder-for-hire, and thirteen counts of money laundering. In return, the government dropped three counts of possession of a firearm by a felon.

Outside the courthouse, Chris Fialko, Steve's attorney, told reporters that the remaining defendants in the case "need to understand that if they choose to go to trial, Steve will testify against them."

Chambers's cooperation may have had the desired effect. By the end of the week, six more defendants followed suit. Robert Chambers, Mary Chambers, Amy Payne, Dennis Floyd, John Hodge, and David Craig all signed agreements in which they pleaded guilty to one count of money laundering.

The two remaining big fish—Kelly Campbell and David Ghantt—joined the list late in the summer.

At a court hearing on September 3, Kelly pleaded guilty to bank larceny and money laundering. She agreed to testify in related trials if asked by prosecutors, who in return dropped a charge of accessory after the fact. After the plea, her lawyer,

Jeff Diamant

James Gronquist, blamed his client's involvement in the heist on the "magnetic personality" of Steve Chambers.

A week later, on September 11, the man who made it all happen pleaded guilty to bank larceny and two counts of money laundering. "I regret that I got entangled in circumstances that led to pain to my wife and to my family," David Ghantt told the judge, as his parents and wife watched him.

⋈

Meanwhile, in Colorado, the Calloways seemed on the verge of criminal success.

During the summer of 1998, Jody's mother, Kathy Grigg, traveled from North Carolina to Littleton to visit her son. Kathy was upset about the arrests of her daughter Amy and son-in-law Nathan; the couple had married in April 1998, the month after their arrests. While talking with Jody about it in Colorado, Kathy noticed he seemed worried about something himself.

His revelation flabbergasted Kathy. He asked his mother if he should return the money.

"It's too late," Kathy said. "You should just keep it now."

Jody would soon give his mother $28,000. A month later, he told his woodworking partner, Joseph Hamilton, about the real source of the $50,000 he had given him earlier in the year. Jody had driven the two of them in his Chevy Tahoe to a storage facility, picked up a large black box, and returned to his home in Littleton. Opening the box, he showed Hamilton over $1 million worth of ones, fives, tens, and twenties. At first, he had said

214

it came from repairing air compressors back in North Carolina. When Hamilton doubted him, Jody admitted he'd stolen it. Now he wanted Hamilton to help him convert it to new bills.

"I don't want to be involved with this," Joseph said.

"You're already involved," Jody responded. "The fifty grand I gave you? That's Loomis Fargo money. The money orders we've purchased? That was Loomis Fargo money. Whether you want to be involved or not, you're involved."

A week later, Jody unleashed his sinister side on a visit to Hamilton in the woodworking shop. "Have you thought about what we talked about?" he asked.

Joseph said he didn't want to be involved.

"If you think about saying anything to anybody about any of this," Jody quickly responded, "your family and yourself are dead."

≍

A new defendant appeared on November 3 and pleaded guilty the same day she was charged. It was Sally Stowe Abernathy, who had sold the house at 503 Stuart Ridge to Steve and Michele for $635,000. She was charged with not filing the IRS paperwork that is required whenever a business receives more than $10,000 in cash, which had happened when Steve and Michele paid her approximately $40,000 for interior design work in their new home.

By early November 1998, eighteen of the twenty-one defendants had pleaded guilty. And prosecutors expected Michael and Kim Goodman to become the nineteenth and twentieth.

But the twenty-first defendant, Jeffrey Guller, seemed headed to trial. Guller hoped that he could beat the case and therefore maintain his legal practice. He stood to face more time than some of the people who'd actually stolen the money, who, by pleading guilty, had qualified for reduced sentences. He understood that's how the system worked but felt he hadn't done anything criminal and was determined to continue practicing law.

Guller's situation was the talk of Gaston County's legal community. His colleagues in Gastonia didn't know if he was guilty or not, but they weren't surprised he wouldn't accept a plea. Guller had a courthouse reputation for feistiness, a blunt speaking style, and a steely face that could hold its own in a mobster movie. His previous battles with the law and the state bar association had wounded him but never knocked him out.

He was known also for his love of sailing and nature photography, as well as for cursing more than your average southern gentleman attorney. Sometimes, when a prosecutor would refuse to let a Guller client plead guilty to a reduced charge, meaning the case was bound for trial, Guller would whip a golf tee from his shirt pocket, hold it in front of the prosecutor's face, and say in a challenging tone, "Tee that motherfucker up! Tee it up!"

He would demonstrate this tack to fellow defense attorneys in the courthouse hallway, sticking his arms out like he was gripping a golf club, staring at the ground in front of him, and yelling, "Tee that motherfucker up! Tee it up!"

Of course, when teed up, the federal government can be a foe to be reckoned with. In early November, shortly before the Goodmans would plead guilty, prosecutors applied more pressure to them and to Guller by adding counts that weren't related to any newfound wrongdoing. The defense lawyers complained, to no avail, that the new indictments were unfair intimidation tactics designed to pressure their clients to plead guilty. The Goodmans would eventually do so. Guller, on the other hand, continued preparing for his trial, which was less than two months away.

A Revealing Trial

The trial of Jeff Guller began January 4, 1999, and was a landmark event in the Loomis case for three reasons. It would be the first time a defendant would test the strength of the government's evidence. It would be the first time Steve Chambers and Kelly Campbell would speak publicly about their experiences. And it would allow the first up-close look at how a defendant had handled Steve Chambers's offer of cash in return for storing heist money—an offer he made to a dozen people in various ways. The others had all pleaded guilty and therefore didn't have to testify.

Among the government witnesses would be Steve Chambers and Kelly Campbell. Up until now, Chambers's portrayals in the media had been built mostly through bizarre passages from FBI affidavits and photographs in jail uniforms. The same was true for Campbell. But as government witnesses in Guller's trial, they would be on display as never before, speaking of their misadventures in public for the first time.

Steve was the government's first witness. After giving a brief description of his own crimes, and pinning the ideas for the theft and murder plot on Kelly, he told the jurors that Guller had first represented him on a larceny charge, and that he occasionally asked Guller for advice on loan-sharking.

He recounted bringing two bags containing $433,000 in cash to Guller's office in the weeks after the heist, for a down payment on his house. Guller, he testified, had suggested he use checks instead. But Steve kept the bags at Guller's office when he left that day, testifying that he retrieved them in early December 1997, and that Guller had taken out $10,000 at Steve's suggestion. When Guller saw the cash, he was "nonchalant," Steve said.

"Why did you leave it with him for that period?" asked Assistant U.S. Attorney Brian Whisler.

"I had fourteen million dollars," Steve said. "I was looking for somewhere to hide it, so I didn't have a problem with leaving that much with Mr. Guller, as I figured it was a safe place to hide and get rid of a half-million dollars."

Steve also testified about his other post-heist business ventures, which he said he'd discussed with Guller.

"Why were you interested in buying a furniture store at this time?" the prosecutor asked.

"Me and Mr. Guller had talked about it, as far as would it be good to have a business to run the money through," Steve told the jury. "That way, it wouldn't attract too much attention, as far as cash deposits going into bank accounts."

"Let's be specific," Whisler said. "Who made these statements?

Did you make these statements? Or did he make these statements about the purpose of having a business?"

"I'd asked him as far as, 'Would it be better to have a business to run cash money through?' And ultimately, he said, 'Yes, of course.' That way...we could put the money into the bank accounts in cash form, and there wouldn't be a lot of questions asked. As far as him coming out and saying, 'You need to go out and buy a business,' no, he did not say that."

Steve discussed the potential deal to buy Crickets. He said he told Guller that he planned to pay the current owner $450,000, some $200,000 of which would be in cash. The paperwork would show the deal being worth only $250,000. He testified that they discussed setting up a corporation that would oversee the house, the furniture business, and the nightclub, and that Michele would be president and Guller would be vice president. Steve wouldn't be listed as an officer due to his felony conviction, which would prevent the club from securing a liquor license. That was why he wanted the pardon and why he discussed with Guller the possibility of paying someone connected in the state capital as much as $250,000 to get it. He had viewed this as a potential bribe, Steve said.

The gist of his testimony was that although he never mentioned the money's origin to Guller, it should've been obvious. At the very least, Steve made it clear to his attorney that he was trying to skirt the law, and Guller indicated a willingness to advise him. The unconsummated deals over the bribe and nightclub didn't relate directly to the substance of Guller's money-laundering charges, but Judge William Osteen told jurors they could decide from the facts whether there were indications that Guller knew Steve's money was dirty.

To devastating effect, the government also played tapes of conversations between Guller and Steve. The jury heard Guller say he would draw up an agreement reflecting Steve's desire to keep a $20,000 deal with Mike Staley "under the table."

Guller had two of Charlotte's best-known lawyers on his side—Harold Bender, who had defended televangelist Jim Bakker in a famous trial on fraud charges in 1989, and Calvin Murphy. During the cross-examination, Murphy tried to discredit Steve Chambers as a witness, attempting to show the jury he was a terrible human being and a lying schemer who was smart enough to con others, including Guller, into believing him.

"I wouldn't say I'm too smart," Steve told Murphy. "If I was, I probably wouldn't be sitting where I'm sitting right now."

Murphy had Steve describe his earlier life as a bookmaker, after establishing that bookmaking and gambling accounted for two-thirds of Steve's income in the mid-1990s. "Now, tell us about bookmaking," Murphy asked. "What do you do?"

"What do you *do*?"

"Yeah. What is involved?"

"Bookmaking is, people lay bets with you on ball games—football, baseball, basketball. [You] go by the point spread, over and under. Depends on what they want to bet, how much they want to bet, how many teams they want to bet on."

Murphy also had Steve recount the substance of his fraud convictions. Basically, Steve told the jury, he had used phony names to open tiny accounts at area banks and then cashed phony checks on the accounts. In an unrelated tax scam, he made money by filing tax returns under false names.

In another exchange, Murphy led Steve to describe a phony business name in the paperwork for Kelly Campbell's minivan purchase, a transaction for which Steve had been present. "Now, on that application, did it ask you for the name of your employer?"

"Yes, it does," Chambers said.

"And what was your response to that?"

"Chambers Industries."

"What is Chambers Industries?"

"I like to call it an industry. It's better than saying Chambers Bookmaking or anything like that. So I come up with Chambers Industries."

Then Murphy asked about the murder plot. "Do you recall telling Mr. McKinney that he could walk up to Mr. Ghantt with a silencer on the gun and just shoot him and keep walking?"

"Yes, we had that conversation," Steve said.

The cross-examination ended with Murphy noting that Steve's plea bargain allowed him the prospect of a reduced sentence in exchange for government testimony. "Now, tell us, Mr. Chambers, what you would do for your freedom."

"What would I *do*?"

"What acts would you engage in, what conduct would you engage in, for the sake of your freedom?"

"I don't think I follow you here."

"Would you steal for your freedom?"

"Yes, I probably would."

"Would you lie for your freedom?"

"Yes, I probably would."

"Would you deceive for your freedom?"

"Yes, I probably would."

"But today," Murphy deadpanned, "you have been truthful, correct?"

"Yes, I have."

When the cross-examination ended, Whisler took the floor again and asked Steve why he had assumed Guller knew the source of the money.

"When I called Mr. Guller up to help Kelly out as far as the FBI questioning her about a polygraph test, I had spoken to Mr. Guller about that. That was right in the first week of October, after Kelly had been interviewed after the robbery. And Mr. Guller had said that he would handle the case for her. I paid him five hundred dollars down to talk to the FBI, to keep the FBI away from her. Kelly went to be interviewed by Mr. Guller. And then, of course, later on, I ended up purchasing the $635,000 home."

"Anything else?"

"Well, it just led me to believe that Mr. Guller knew where the funds came from. I don't think it took a rocket scientist to figure that out. That's my opinion."

Kelly Campbell was the next government witness. The prosecutor began by having her acknowledge her frequent marijuana use before her arrest, knowing Guller's lawyers might bring it up anyway. He then had her recount how, after the heist, Steve set her up with Guller for the call to the FBI.

During the cross-examination, when Harold Bender asked her to recount more details of the heist planning, she said the theft had been Steve's idea, contradicting Steve, who had pinned it on her.

"Steve Chambers was the brains? The mastermind?"

"Yes."

"Steve Chambers called the shots?"

"Yes, he did… He made all of the plans of how the money was going to be taken care of, where it was going to be hid. He had control of all the money. He made all of the plans as to how to carry it out. He said who got what."

Of course, Kelly and Steve had both played key roles in the plot's development. But the prosecutor, perhaps worried that the government's two witnesses had contradicted each other, asked Kelly again about her pot use. She had started smoking it around age thirteen, she said, and at the time of the heist she was smoking about three joints a day.

"It got to a point where I was smoking pot like most people smoke cigarettes," she said.

"Just a minute," the judge said. "When you say, 'Like most people smoke cigarettes,' I don't really know whether most people smoke cigarettes or not, but assuming they do, what do you mean by that?"

Kelly said, "When I'd get up in the morning, I would smoke a joint. If I was going to go shopping, I had to smoke a joint. I felt like I couldn't function unless I was stoned."

≍

The next government witness, Guller's former office assistant, offered more damaging testimony. Jennifer Norman told the jurors that she and the office secretary had grown suspicious over Steve and Michele's ability to buy the $635,000 house, given that Guller had just represented Steve on false-check charges. Then, when she saw Steve's bags of money, she was certain it came from the Loomis Fargo heist. She said she told Guller this and that she even mentioned the reward that was announced on *America's Most Wanted*. But Guller had told her she couldn't prove it, she testified.

After a few more questions from Whisler, she said this: "He told me that he didn't really care where the money came from. He was getting paid. And in the law office, I mean, he let a lot of people finance out—you know, pay down and whatever. And Steve was always one to pay up front, and so his comment was, 'I don't care. I get paid.' Because like I said, Steve was always one to pay up front. He paid his bill."

Norman also told jurors that she actually placed a call to *America's Most Wanted* about Steve Chambers but was basically blown off, because the only suspect at that time was David Ghantt.

In the cross-examination, Murphy had Norman acknowledge that she lacked legal or paralegal training, and that Guller had never discussed *any* of his clients with her; therefore, it wasn't significant that he hadn't engaged her in conversation about Steve Chambers.

⋝⋜

The next government witness was John Hodge, the sixty-nine-year-old father of Calvin Hodge. Both father and son had pleaded guilty to money laundering. John Hodge spoke in an extremely high-pitched voice and was clearly proud to be participating in such a distinguished courtroom setting, even while recounting his deeds of questionable repute.

He told the jury that Steve Chambers had asked him after the heist to secure a $100,000 check for him. Steve would give Hodge that amount in cash, plus a fee, and Hodge would then use money from his personal account to get Steve the check. Hodge had refused Steve's request for the $100,000 check but agreed to one for $80,000. In return for that, Steve paid him a 10 percent fee that equaled $8,000. Soon afterward, he asked Hodge to get him another check, this one for $62,000, for Steve's mobile-home purchase. Hodge's fee was 10 percent for this check also, bringing his total in fees to $14,200.

Keesler asked, "What did you think about the fact that Mr. Chambers was going to pay you money to go get these checks?"

"Well," Hodge told the jurors, with nothing but earnestness in his voice, "years ago, I used to be what you call a speculator and a 'ten percenter,' if any of you is familiar with either one of them. And that's where you would do something, and they would pay you ten percent for doing it, and that was my purpose of doing the transaction is the ten percent, and not knowing any more about the situation than what it was. But I personally wouldn't do it again under the circumstances, any circumstances."

If the jury hadn't been watching Keesler for his response to this perhaps overly honest answer from his own witness, he likely would've covered his face in his hands.

Another witness, FBI agent Bart Boodee, testified about his interviews with Guller after the heist arrests. He described how Guller changed his story about the cash sitting in his office after Boodee had mentioned that lying to the FBI was a felony. Boodee said that, at first, Guller told him the cash had been in his office only briefly. But then, after Boodee's "reminder," Guller acknowledged it was there for weeks, and that before he returned it, Steve told him to withdraw some money as a gratuity for holding it. Guller told Boodee that he declined the offer at first, the agent testified, but he finally partook, taking $10,000 for himself.

John Wydra was the final prosecution witness. Using an elaborate computer display projected onto a screen, he outlined the transactions Guller performed or had discussed performing for Steve. All told, Wydra showed the jury a figure of $1.2 million that "Chambers had available to him with Guller's knowledge."

Among the first defense witnesses was Lurie Limbaugh, who Steve had stolen from in 1994. Guller's attorneys were attempting to impeach Steve's credibility as a witness. During his testimony, Steve had downplayed the charge against him that year as a drug deal gone bad, but the defense wanted to prove not only that he'd been lying, but also that he was good at getting regular people to trust him. Limbaugh said she had met Steve at a Gastonia club, and that he offered to help her purchase a car. She took him up on it and mentioned she had $3,000 in her purse. While they were parked in a vehicle, he grabbed the money and ran away, she said.

If Limbaugh had trusted Steve enough to be alone with him with $3,000 after knowing him such a short time, the defense attorneys seemed to be asking, was it so far-fetched for Guller to have believed that Chambers's money came from legal gambling proceeds?

Next on the witness stand was a well-known figure in Charlotte, former mayor Richard Vinroot. He and Guller were friends from childhood who attended the same public schools, college, and law school. They even served as co-captains of the high-school football team.

"My opinion is that he has the highest integrity," Vinroot told jurors.

During the cross-examination, Keesler asked, "Mr. Vinroot, you don't know anything about the underlying facts of this case, do you?"

"Absolutely nothing about it," the former mayor said. "I have, frankly, not kept up with it because I was so hurt by the allegations, of course, and worried about my friend."

Next, two of Guller's Gaston County colleagues, Max Childers and Calvin Hamrick—the latter a former district attorney—also told jurors Guller was a man of integrity. They admitted knowing little, if anything, of his state-bar reprimands.

And Guller's wife, Brenda, took the stand next and said Jeff was a very good stepfather to her children from a previous marriage.

≥≤

Guller himself was the defense's most important witness. He took the stand after his wife, on January 7, 1999. Describing his background, he spoke of his 1966 law degree from the University of North Carolina at Chapel Hill, his work as a prosecutor in the late 1960s, his six months of active duty in the National Guard, and his leadership roles in the Gaston County March of Dimes, the Red Cross, the Young Lawyers Association, and his synagogue.

He said he had met Steve Chambers in 1995 to discuss the 1994 larceny charge. Steve told him he worked in Charlotte and made $11.50 an hour at a company named Hydrovac, where he had allegedly been employed for six years. Guller had no reason not to believe him, he said. In November 1995, Steve hadn't shown up for a court date and the judge issued a warrant for his arrest.

The next time Steve and Guller met was in the summer of 1997, when Steve went to see him about the worthless-check charges.

"What was his attitude when he came to see you?" Murphy asked.

"He seemed a little put out with me about the larceny warrant, about why I didn't get it handled," Guller testified. "I got a little put out with him and said, 'Where the hell were you? I can't deal with your case unless you come to court, and I'm not going to deal with your case unless you pay me.'"

"What was his response or reaction to that?"

"He said, 'Fine, fine, we will work everything out,' and I said okay."

Murphy asked, "Did he ever talk to you about bookmaking, loan-sharking, gambling, anything like that?"

"Never, other than the fact about his Atlantic City [trips]," Guller said. He mentioned the bag of cash Chambers brought to the closing and testified that he told Steve that using it would require taking the cash to the bank to fill out paperwork about the money's source. "He didn't appear to want to do that," Guller told the jury. "I said, 'Why not?' I said, 'If it's valid money, if you won it like you said, it's already reported, so why not?'"

The defendant said he told Chambers to bring him other funds, and soon, or they would have to deposit the cash in the bank to close on the house. He also said he asked Chambers how he could afford the house. "He said that he had won a great deal of money gambling in Atlantic City," Guller testified.

Murphy asked if he pursued the matter any further.

"I did," Guller said. "I asked him how much he won, and he didn't say. He just said, 'A lot of money, more than enough to buy this house.'"

He contended he had no reason to suspect Steve was involved with the Loomis heist. "This thing was reported as maybe the second-biggest robbery in the United States. Chambers? No way did Chambers have sense enough to do something like this... I had no idea what he won in Atlantic City."

Steve eventually brought Guller checks to pay for the house, so Guller never had to deposit the $433,000 in the bank. But he acknowledged taking $10,000 from the bag before returning it to Steve. He said Steve told him to take that amount several times before he agreed, and that he did so only because Steve called it a Christmas gift.

"[Chambers] called me and said, 'Things went real well, and I appreciate what you did.' I said, 'Fine, thank you.' He said, 'I want you to take $10,000.' And I said, 'No, I'm not taking $10,000.' He said, 'I want you to take $10,000.' I said, 'We'll see.' So I didn't do anything. He called me another time and said, 'Have you taken your $10,000?' And I said no. 'I want you to take $10,000.' I said, 'Okay, we'll see.' And I didn't. And when he called and asked for the money back, he said, 'Have you taken your $10,000?' I said no. He said, 'I want you to take $10,000.' He said, 'Christmas is coming, take the $10,000.' I said okay."

Then he recounted a proposed land deal involving Kelly Campbell's husband, in which Guller said he would help Steve put the land under a phony name. In giving his testimony, Guller unwittingly riled the judge.

Murphy asked, "Did you ever tell [Steve] that you could put it in a fictitious name?"

"I may have said 'Yeah' or 'Okay,' just to get him off the phone."

"Did you have any intentions of doing that?"

"Absolutely not. I wouldn't do that for anybody."

"Did he ever bring any specific documents to you…?"

"Just a minute," Judge Osteen interrupted, facing Guller. "Why would you have said that to get him off the phone?"

"A lot of times," Guller said, "when I'm talking to somebody, a client or whoever, and he's told me what he needed to tell me, that he wanted me to do some work, and then he just starts talking, and I have got another line holding or I have got somewhere else I've got to be or I've got something else to do, I just want to be off the phone."

His answer appalled the judge. "Isn't he, at that time, asking you about some legal advice? 'Will you put it in an assumed name?' That's legal advice he is asking you for, isn't it?"

Guller said, "I think I've gotten the gist of what he wanted to say by then, and that was an opportunity where he just took to talk, and he liked to talk big about things that he could do."

"All right, sir," the judge said. "Proceed, Mr. Murphy."

Keesler, in perhaps the most devastating part of his cross-examination, insinuated that Guller would've had to be an absolute dolt not to realize the source of Steve's money. Citing the testimony of Jennifer Norman, who of course had called *America's Most Wanted*, he reminded Guller—and the jurors—that Norman had considerably less formal education than he did.

"You have a college and law degree, don't you?" Keesler asked.

"Yes, sir," Guller said.

"And you're a practicing lawyer for thirty years?"

"Yes."

"And none of this clicked for you, I take it?"

"No, sir."

"You didn't see anything unusual about it at all."

"No, sir."

⋇

During his closing argument to the jurors, Harold Bender maintained that Guller simply didn't know where the money came from. "If his client lies to him, how is he supposed to know? If Mr. Guller's client says, 'I won a whole lot of money in Atlantic City,' does Mr. Guller say, 'I don't believe you. Get out of my office'?"

As for Steve Chambers, Bender said, "There's not a truthful bone in that man's body. He involved his parents. He involved his in-laws. He involved his friends. He's a user. He's a manipulator. He's the government's primary witness."

Parts of Guller's testimony could have inspired reasonable doubt against the government's case, if the jurors believed his point of view. But he seemed uncooperative to the prosecutor on the witness stand and appeared to be lying when he said he didn't suspect that Steve was involved in the heist. And on the tapes, he sounded like an aider and abettor to Chambers; at the very least, he sounded indifferent.

The jury took just four hours in the late afternoon on January 8, 1999, to send back its verdicts: guilty on all six counts, five of them for money laundering and one for conspiracy to commit money laundering.

Selling Elvis

Public fascination over the heist reached such heights that on February 20, 1999, about five thousand people crowded the Metrolina Expo flea market in Charlotte for the government's auction of seized items believed to have been bought with heist loot. Federal auctions like this typically attract little public notice, but this one drew advance newspaper coverage, *People* magazine, and network TV crews.

In the days leading up to it, callers across the country had phoned in asking about the velvet Elvis, by now a symbol of what made the heist narrative so funny to so many people. Without its infamous context, the Elvis was worth about thirty dollars, but the auctioneer expected it to bring as much as $1,000. Among other attention-grabbing items up for sale were a blue barrel that Steve Chambers used to store money, Michele's BMW, a silver cigar holder engraved with Steve Chambers's name, statues, paintings, and the six-foot wooden Indian.

The steady hum of laughter in the auction space grew louder when Manny Fisher, the bespectacled, gray-haired auctioneer, announced that the blue barrel was up for bid. Like the velvet Elvis, it was worth maybe thirty dollars brand new but was clearly going to fetch more—perhaps $100, some speculated, or $150 if someone really wanted a souvenir.

The bidding shot up to $500 in less than thirty seconds. It kept rising—$600, then $700. Even Fisher, who expected some antics today, couldn't believe where it was going. Eight hundred dollars, then $900, then, finally, $1,050 from the owner of a Charlotte recycling company, who would proudly place it in her front office.

The crowd cheered again when Fisher raised the velvet Elvis in his arms. Bids shot past $1,200, then $1,300, and it finally sold for $1,600 to Tom Shaw, the owner of the American Gun and Pawn Shop on South Boulevard, where it would hang for the publicity. Shaw even received a certificate of authenticity that the piece was a "seized asset from the $17 million Loomis Fargo robbery."

Most people at the auction spent lesser amounts on small statues, paintings, or knickknacks from Steve and Michele's house, or on furniture seized from their store. The owner of a publicity company spent $32,000 on Michele's BMW, about $1,500 less than it was worth, planning to donate it to a children's charity he owned, which would then raffle it off. Eric Payne's Harley-Davidson sold for $16,000.

In all, the auction raised $360,000, all of it destined for Loomis Fargo and its insurance company, Lloyd's of London.

Two months earlier, Steve and Michele's criminally acquired house had sold for $486,000 to a doctor, his wife, and their children. The companies remained about $2 million in the hole.

≥≤

On January 20, 1999, Philip Noel Johnson was sentenced to twenty-five years in prison for stealing $18.8 million from Loomis Fargo in Florida and holding up his colleagues at gunpoint twenty-two months earlier.

The defendants in the North Carolina heist expected far less time behind bars, because they did not use, or threaten to use, weapons during the theft. Technically, they did not "rob" anybody, since the term "robbery" implies the use or threat of force. No one, therefore, was charged with robbery; instead, the defendants faced charges of bank larceny, which carried a maximum sentence of ten years, in addition to money laundering, which had a maximum sentence of twenty years. Their guilty pleas and—generally speaking—their insignificant prior criminal records would likely mean their prison sentences would be far shorter than the maximums.

On February 23, 1999, six of the defendants walked into the federal courthouse on Trade Street to learn their punishments. Perusing a paper sentencing grid that used current and past convictions as a guide for each crime, Judge Graham Mullen sentenced Scott Grant to four years and seven months in prison and ordered him to pay $26,000 in restitution. The judge sentenced Eric Payne, who had spent much more heist money than Grant, to six and a half years in prison and ordered him to pay $292,000 in restitution. A portion of whatever money they made when freed would go to Loomis Fargo and its insurance company, until both were fully reimbursed.

"Mr. Payne, I realize there's probably no way on God's green earth you can pay back $292,000," Judge Mullen told him. "The law requires that I impose that."

"I made a bad mistake," Payne said. "And Lord knows, I would take it back."

The longest sentence of the day, eleven years and three months, went to Mike McKinney. The shortest went to Sandra Floyd, Dennis Floyd, and Calvin Hodge, each of whom received three years of probation. In addition, Hodge was sentenced to spend four months under house arrest and to perform one hundred hours of community service.

Michele Chambers came to court to watch her parents' sentencing. She knew they wouldn't have been there if not for her, and she cried and hugged her sister when Mullen announced probation instead of prison for the Floyds, who held each other's hands as the judge spoke. Brian Whisler, the prosecutor, told the judge the Floyds had been the most forthcoming of all the defendants in the case.

The next day, two more defendants—John Hodge and David Craig—each received two years of probation on their money-laundering convictions. Hodge's lawyer, James Gray, cracked up the courtroom when he revealed that his client had actually declared the $14,200 paid to him by Chambers as income on his tax return. After the court hearing, Hodge told the *Charlotte Observer* he considered it a "service" to buy the checks for Chambers.

"I didn't have any reason to doubt that it [was] legitimate money," he said. "Nowadays, you never know who has $100,000 or $150,000 available."

Regrets

The search continued for the missing $2.6 million.

Loomis' insurance company, Lloyd's of London, wasn't relying on the FBI to find it. It had hired an investigative firm called Amsec International, whose investigator, Joel Bartow, interviewed defendants about the whereabouts of the money. Bartow's job could be dirty. Sometimes, he drove outside the homes of Michele Chambers and the Floyds, placed their road-side garbage bags in his trunk, and drove elsewhere to examine them. He tried the same tactic outside the home of Robert and Mary Chambers, but every time he approached their home in his car they came to the window and his cover was blown. He discovered paperwork indicating Michele Chambers had rented a storage facility that the FBI didn't know about, but all it contained were a few inexpensive household goods.

During his interviews, he encountered Dennis Floyd, who, when pressed, mentioned that his stepdaughter Michele had some jewelry hidden in the house. Shortly thereafter, the FBI recovered the $43,000 diamond ring, after Bartow and Floyd persuaded Michele that returning it was in everybody's interest. When Michele handed it to John Wydra at the FBI's Charlotte headquarters, the agent asked without missing a beat, "Where's the Rolex?" She answered that she had sold it, but she also returned the diamond tennis bracelet.

On March 9, 1999, the government asked a judge to revoke Michele's bond and return her to jail until her trial. Not only had she concealed the ring, but she also was accused of violating several other conditions of her bond, including associating with someone involved in unlawful conduct—a new boyfriend who had an altercation with police, for which Michele was present.

Her lawyer, Andy Culler, argued that Michele shouldn't be penalized for her boyfriend's behavior, but he didn't strongly contest the government's request. Judge Horn returned Michele to jail on March 11. At the hearing, Culler asked the judge to ensure that, while in jail, she received medication for back pain, anxiety, and depression.

Meanwhile, the sentencings continued. On March 29, Steve's parents, convicted of money laundering for renting safe-deposit boxes, learned that they would stay out of prison but be confined to their home for five months. After this house arrest, they each would be on probation for two years and seven months. It was a more severe sentence than that given to Michele's parents, who each got off with just probation.

"They don't deserve prison," said David Phillips, the lawyer for Steve's parents. "They still love their son, even though their son got them in trouble."

On April 27, Amy Grant—formerly Amy Grigg, before her marriage to Nathan about a year earlier—was sentenced to eighteen months in prison, with the option of shortening it to six months if she served it in a prison boot camp. The judge, scheduled to sentence Nathan Grant two days later, agreed to stagger their sentences so that one of them could always be living with their children; they had welcomed their second child into the world a month earlier.

In 1976, a few months after French master thief Albert Spaggiari led the $8 million bank theft in Nice and treated his associates to an elegant meal in the vault, he was captured. Every Thursday for several weeks, he was questioned in a second-floor room in the courthouse. On March 10, 1977, after complaining of a toothache and walking toward the window, he jumped out. Shocked investigators and guards ran to the window just in time to see the former paratrooper land easily on a car roof and hop on the back of a waiting motorcycle, which drove him away. He was not seen in person again until his death in 1989—when his body was delivered to his mother's house—though he is believed to have sent money to the owner of the car whose roof he damaged on the jump.

David Ghantt and Steve Chambers, led into court in prison garb and shackles, attempted no such theatrics at their sentencing hearings on April 29, 1999. Steve read an apology from a piece of paper. "I wish I could take back that October night, but I can't," he said. "I don't know if I can get over the hurt I've caused my children from being greedy… I lost sight of what's important in life, which are hugs and kisses from my kids."

Before testifying for the government at Guller's trial, Steve was slotted to receive a sentence of fifteen to nineteen years. But the prosecutor now recommended a lesser sentence, eleven years and three months. "We believe his testimony was helpful to secure the government conviction of Mr. Guller at the trial," Brian Whisler told the judge.

Steve Chambers thought he deserved an even lighter sentence, given that he also had confessed right after his arrests. Chris Fialko, his lawyer, pushed for seven and a half years. But Judge Mullen sided with the prosecutor, opting for the same sentence given to Mike McKinney, and also ordered that Steve pay $3.8 million in restitution.

Next up for the judge's consideration was David Ghantt. The judge smiled as Ghantt stood up and stuck out his chest, as if concerned to display proper posture. "Your Honor, if I could undo what I did, I would," David said. "I see how I hurt my wife and my family. I'm sorry for what I did. I was stuck in a go-nowhere job… I was unhappy with my life. I worked a lot of hours. It's no excuse for what I did. I'm sorry."

Mullen sentenced David to seven and a half years in prison and the payment of $3.8 million in restitution. It was no surprise he received less time than Steve, who had much more control of the stolen money after the theft and who, after all, had plotted to kill him.

Nobody expected that David Ghantt, Kelly Campbell, or Steve Chambers would ever pay off their restitution. They would be lucky if more of the missing money was found, or if the others were somehow able to pay it off. If that happened, they wouldn't be liable for it anymore. But it seemed likely they would be writing restitution checks for the rest of their lives.

During the same court session in which Ghantt and Chambers were sentenced, Judge Mullen sentenced Nathan Grant to three years and one month in prison and Amy Payne to a year of work release plus two years of probation. Each would also pay restitution.

In June and September, two people were sentenced who, in retrospect, could have received lesser penalties had they made different decisions after their arrests. Jeff Guller received eight years in prison, and it wasn't lost on him that this was a heavier punishment than that given to the man who actually stole the money.

"I will survive, and I will be back," Guller said in court. "And I will be a citizen of this country that works hard and…accomplishes something." He said he rued the day Steve Chambers first came into his office. "I'm not a money launderer," Guller said. "Nor would I ever conspire with a thief like him."

In the summer of 1999, the North Carolina State Bar would disbar Guller, to nobody's surprise.

Also to nobody's surprise, given her recent bond revocation, Michele Chambers was sentenced in September to seven years and eight months in prison—the fourth-most-severe sentence in the case, after her husband's, Mike McKinney's, and Guller's. She was also ordered to pay $4.8 million in restitution. Judge Mullen recommended that while imprisoned she receive mental-health treatment.

The sentence was a compromise. The government wanted nine years, and Michele's lawyer suggested seven years and three months. Andy Culler told the judge his client had had a difficult personal life due to her parents' divorce, a teenage pregnancy, and various medical conditions. But Brian Whisler told the court her personal history was irrelevant here.

"There are many people with those factors who don't resort to crime," he said.

The last main defendant to be sentenced, Kelly Campbell, received five years and ten months. She was ordered to pay $4.7 million in restitution.

Kelly wept in court and apologized, saying she had come to realize that religion and family were more important than money. "I'd gotten too far away from the Lord, and He had to do something to wake me up," she told the judge.

Mullen seemed moved. "It's always refreshing to the court to hear someone fess up and take their medicine." He ordered that her sentence not begin until January 2000, so she could spend Christmas at home with her children—under house arrest.

Out West

The New Year brought little change to the case. Each of the twenty-one defendants had already been convicted and sentenced. John Wydra and other FBI agents had mostly moved on to other cases, relegating the Loomis heist to almost a hobby status. Though about $1.5 million in Loomis cash remained missing, the case was largely solved, from the agency's perspective.

That said, Wydra still hoped to find the missing money. He had secured a list of names of everyone who had opened accounts at Lincoln Self Storage, the place where Steve Chambers said the money had disappeared. Among the names on it was Jennifer Calloway, and a records search revealed she had once shared an address with Nathan and Amy Grant, both of whom had admitted hiding Steve's stolen money in a different locker at Lincoln Self Storage. But the normal course of new cases coming their way left Wydra and the other agents little time to investigate the match.

Of course, the victim companies—Loomis Fargo and its

insurance company, Lloyd's of London—desperately wanted the money found. Lloyd's was still paying Amsec International to try to find it. The people at Amsec figured the FBI now had higher crime-fighting priorities, so they increased their own efforts.

Robert Osborne Jr., of Amsec, interviewed Michele and Steve Chambers in prison, separately, to check their credibility on the Lincoln Self Storage theft. Both mentioned Nathan Grant as having helped them stash the missing money.

Osborne wanted to travel to Beckley, West Virginia, to talk to both Grant brothers, who were imprisoned there. He struggled to gain access because he wasn't a law-enforcement officer, but the FBI helped arrange his clearance.

Before Osborne had a chance to talk with the Grants, he learned exciting news from a prison official there. Months earlier, another inmate had mentioned that one of the Grant boys had been bragging that he had money waiting for him when he left prison—money from the heist. The inmate thought that sharing the information would win him time off his sentence. But until Osborne's trip, nobody passed it on.

Two weeks later, Nathan Grant told Osborne that his wife's half brother, Jody Calloway, supposedly had the missing money. For more information, Osborne needed to talk to Amy Grant and her mother, Kathy Grigg.

On August 23, Osborne and another Amsec employee, Jamie Waters, arrived at Amy and Kathy's home in Maiden, North Carolina. Only Amy was there, as her mother was at a doctor's appointment. But Amy told them she knew about the missing cash. Her mother had told her, during the summer of 1998, that her half brother Jody Calloway had it. Her mother knew more about it than Amy, but Amy was able to provide a few details of her own that helped implicate Jody.

Amy said the amount of cash that she and Nathan had hidden for Steve Chambers scared her so much that she'd told Jody she was storing money for the mob. She let him know it was at Lincoln Self Storage, in case anything happened to her. She suspected that a receipt from the storage facility lying around her home might have led the Calloways to the locker. If the investigators wanted more, they needed to speak to her mother, who Amy had to pick up at the doctor's.

That evening, after Kathy Grigg arrived home, she provided essential details. Jody and Jennifer Calloway had lived with the Grants a while back, but they'd moved from North Carolina to Colorado a few months after the heist. Jody had taken the stolen money from the storage locker and had admitted this to her. She said that Jody had even asked her, his mother, if he should return the money, and that she had told him to keep it. She also said he had given her $28,000 in cash when he visited her months later in North Carolina. Kathy felt bad, like she was betraying him now, and she told the investigators she hoped her cooperation would count in his favor. Both women gave written statements.

Five days later, Osborne returned to the home with John Wydra in tow and had Kathy Grigg read back her statement to double-check its veracity. She told them it was true.

At this point, the word of Kathy Grigg offered the main direct evidence against her son, but circumstantial evidence was growing. Records showed the Calloways lived in a $212,000 home, a considerable improvement from their North Carolina accommodations. Employment tax records showed Jody Calloway had earned $608 during the second quarter of 1998 and $731 during the fourth quarter of 1999. Jennifer Calloway hadn't made much more. Yet according to Department of Motor Vehicle records, they owned five vehicles—a 1998 Ford Explorer, a 1996 Chevy Tahoe, a 1985 Ford Mustang, a 1977 Harley-Davidson, and a 1990 Chris-Craft powerboat. The money to fund those had to be coming from somewhere.

On August 31, 2000, the FBI secretly videotaped a meeting between Amy and Jody, half-siblings, in a Colorado hotel room. Amy told him their mother had told her about his theft from the locker. He angrily denied everything. He even told her he suspected the FBI was watching him as he spoke to her. He also said their mother was crazy. Amy spoke right past him, telling him to return the money and think of the family.

"I don't know nothin' about this bullshit!" Jody yelled. "You need to stop insinuating that I do!"

Jody didn't provide them a smoking-gun confession, but the FBI felt confident enough about the accumulating evidence— not to mention his anger at his half sister in the hotel room—that Wydra arrested him later in the day. In court, a federal magistrate ordered him kept in custody in Englewood, Colorado, without bond. He was subsequently taken to jail in Charlotte, where evidence was building further against both him and his wife, Jennifer.

On October 2, 2000, Brian Whisler argued in court that

Calloway should be kept in jail without bond. He cited the move to Colorado, Calloway's failure to list most of his vehicles on a financial disclosure form after his arrest, and his alleged propensity toward violence. Calloway had been recently charged with felony menacing in Colorado for an alleged road-rage incident involving a gun.

Jody's attorney, Chuck Morgan, contended that the government's evidence was flimsy, and that the couple's Colorado lifestyle came from hard work and savings.

Judge McKnight decided to free Jody Calloway on $150,000 bond, putting him under house arrest in Littleton, Colorado. He ordered Jody to get a job.

Meanwhile, back in Charlotte, a federal grand jury met in November and indicted Jody Calloway for money laundering, his wife for possession of stolen property and money laundering, and his mother for possession of stolen property—the $28,000 she said Calloway had given her.

The FBI also secured warrants for the Calloways' home and vehicles, and on March 5 they seized boxes of paperwork from the home, including closing documents, titles to their vehicles, tax returns for 2000, and pay stubs from the electronic company where Jody had worked. A week later Wydra tried to seize money from the Calloways' bank account, only to learn that Jennifer Calloway had emptied it of $52,000 earlier in the day. As pressure on them increased, she realized she should turn that money over to the government, and did so on May 8, 2001.

⋙⋘

The trial of Jody and Jennifer Calloway began on August 20. On the first day, government witness Steve Chambers recounted paying Nathan Grant and Amy Grigg, then Nathan's fiancée, $70,000 in return for their help hiding millions of dollars at Lincoln Self Storage. Only the three of them had keys to the locker, Steve testified. He recalled their shock in December 1997 to learn that the key didn't work and that the money was missing.

The next day, the government was in for an unpleasant surprise. Kathy Grigg, its star witness, directly contradicted everything she had told Amsec and the FBI on their visit to her home the previous August. Her words baffled the federal prosecutors, who had offered her immunity for truthful testimony. Confronted with the written statement she had signed thirteen months earlier, she insisted to prosecutors that her son never told her he stole the money and never gave her $28,000.

In Kathy's words, when Amsec officials came to her house, "I was frightened and scared, so I told them it was true." She described her medical problems, which included high blood pressure and depression, and said she was sedated during the Amsec interview, having just returned from her doctor.

"I wasn't aware of what I was writing when I wrote it," she said.

That afternoon, as court was closing down, Jody Calloway glared at Joseph Hamilton, who was scheduled to testify the next day. Hamilton, Jody's business partner in Colorado, was also Jennifer Calloway's brother-in-law. Jody's glare frightened Hamilton enough that he wondered what would happen if Jody were free. He knew what he had to do.

On the next day, his surprise testimony against Calloway virtually guaranteed the trial's outcome. In a confession while jurors were outside the courtroom, Hamilton told the judge that in 1998, Jody Calloway had shown him somewhere between $1 million and $1.5 million in cash that had been hidden in a Littleton storage facility. He said Jody had told him that the money came from a heist, that he had taken it from a storage facility in North Carolina, and that "if I [Hamilton] ever thought about saying anything to anyone that 'your family and yourself are dead,'" Hamilton testified.

"Did you think he was serious?" the prosecutor asked.

"Yes," Hamilton said. He said Jennifer had called him after her husband's arrest, asking him to hide the money. So Hamilton had gone to the storage locker and tried to bury the cash where he hunted in the Rocky Mountains. Then, while Jody Calloway was out on bail and freed from house arrest, he and Hamilton dug up most of the money. Hamilton added that he had kept $68,000 buried, and that he realized he was getting himself in trouble by saying that. But he said he was more afraid of what could happen to him if the Calloways were acquitted. He had even finalized his will. "I felt that if they went back to Colorado, my wife, my two boys, and my baby were in danger," he said.

It got worse for the Calloways when Jennifer's sister, Jill Shelly, testified that the previous night over dinner the couple had asked her what she would say on the witness stand. The Calloways, she said, asked her to lie in court and testify she had paid them $700 a month in rent while living in an Arizona condo they owned; her rent money presumably would explain some of the extra cash the Calloways had on hand. But Shelly had never paid them actual rent—only money for utilities, fees, and taxes. After Shelly told her husband about the conversation, he called the authorities.

"He told me the truth was the best possible way," she said. "This is very hard."

Judge Richard Voorhees had heard enough. The Calloways' bonds were revoked, and they were handcuffed and led to jail.

The next day's testimony focused on their lives in Colorado. Their old landlord testified that when Jody Calloway moved to Littleton from North Carolina in January 1998, he paid the rent six months in advance. Another man said he received $4,500 in cash and a $4,000 cashier's check for a boat he sold Jennifer four months later.

Other testimony revealed that the Calloways later bought a house for $212,000, putting $50,000 down in October 1998. And while they had one vehicle while living in North Carolina, in Colorado they had five. Also, that they had written virtually identical resignation letters to their respective employers attributing their move to the other spouse being transferred. Neither was actually transferred, their former supervisors said in court.

≍

In the meantime, FBI agents used Joseph Hamilton's testimony as a map to find more of the missing money. Over the weekend, they discovered $68,000 buried in a tin ammunition container on a mountain near Denver, Colorado, and $10,000 in the ceiling of Hamilton's workshop in Littleton. Agents flew the money to Charlotte so prosecutors would have it in court on the next day of testimony.

As it turned out, it wasn't necessary. Over the weekend, the Calloways and their lawyers concluded that the defendants should plead guilty. On Monday, August 27, 2001, with a bag containing $78,000 sitting on the prosecutor's table ready to be used as evidence, they submitted guilty pleas to money laundering and receiving stolen property, still managing to anger authorities when they said they didn't know the location of the remaining, unspent portion of their loot.

Kathy Grigg continued to maintain she wasn't guilty of possession of stolen property involving the disputed $28,000. The prosecutor charged her with perjury. She agreed to plead guilty in return for the prosecutors' dismissal of the larceny charge. But then she told a *Charlotte Observer* reporter, Aileen Soper, that she was actually innocent. When prosecutors read the newspaper story, they asked a judge to reverse her guilty plea. She went to trial for perjury and lost.

Jody Calloway was sentenced to six and a half years in prison, a heavier punishment than what most of the defendants had received in the earlier rounds of arrests. Jennifer was sentenced to four and a half years, and Kathy Grigg to two years. Their closest personal connections to the original theft, Nathan and Amy Grant, had already completed their sentences by the time the Calloways and Kathy Grigg would start theirs.

At his sentencing hearing on February 3, 2003, Jody Calloway said he thought the money had been from either drug deals or organized crime, and that he had pleaded guilty only because he'd been "under intense pressure." He contended the government was responsible for his situation.

"If these people had come to us in the beginning, besides hunting me and my wife down like we were rabid dogs in the street, we would not have arrived at this point... This perpetual case, it's unreal, and I can't believe I'm in this position."

Epilogue

There was something about David Ghantt that made it hard not to like him.

He had several strikes against him, of course. He was awful to his wife. He abandoned his entire family without so much as a note. He stole a ton of money from his employer, abused a position of trust in the process, and wasn't sorry about it.

And yet, after everything, he emerges as a somewhat sympathetic character in the story just told. Part of this is easy to explain. His accomplices were working to kill him. He spent just a sliver of the amount he stole. The woman he loved didn't love him back. And he'd been stuck in a job he hated.

Without excusing his actions, it's easy for us to imagine experiencing a less dramatic version of what he went through. Most people have had a boss or two who they loathed. Most people have loved someone who didn't love them back and maybe made bad choices as a result. Most people have had their trust betrayed.

For David Ghantt, all these life events happened at the same time, converging in a most remarkable fashion.

And was he bitter about it? No. While interviewed in prison, he exuded the vibe of someone who'd lost a huge bet but had affirmatively decided to be a good sport about it, because he knew the odds had been long in the first place and that what he did was wrong. And he made no bones about his excitement that people will read about him for decades to come.

"It was kind of an ego thing," he told me. "I knew [that] when I did this, I would be famous. I knew it would create a big stir. The thought of that, I think, drives a lot of crimes. People want the fifteen minutes of fame. I doubt my place in the history books will be that big, but people will know me for a while."

He was candid, as well, about his lack of remorse. He said he felt bad about upsetting his wife and family but not about the act itself or the bad publicity it caused Loomis Fargo, which he felt had worked him too hard for too little money. "I'm not gonna be like the other people, crying and weeping about how sorry they are. That's fake… What's the point? I made a choice, a decision. It was a calculated risk. I guess that makes me a bastard of sorts."

He said his time on the run was the most exciting period of his life. And he clearly appreciated that some of his experiences would read well; he enjoyed telling me about listening to the radio while driving to work in his truck on the morning of the crime. "They were playing 'Take the Money and Run,'" he said. "I shit you not."

While David's tale offered the most compelling personal narrative of any of the thieves, the prolonged public intrigue over the Loomis Fargo heist owes more, perhaps, to fascination over a simple question: could they still have gotten away with it if they'd been more careful?

In some ways, the answer seems obvious. To get away with it, they could have spent less or moved far away so they'd have been more difficult to track down. Had the Chamberses been willing to leave the area, rather than immediately buying a $635,000 home that was even nearer to the scene of the crime than was their previous abode, maybe they could have thrown their money around without raising the alarms that eventually led informants in the Charlotte area to contact the FBI. And if they'd needed to stay in the Charlotte area, they could have waited longer (much longer) to change residences and refrained from showing bags of cash to people they didn't know very well. They made plenty of mistakes.

Still, even without mistakes, the cards were stacked against this group from the very beginning, mainly due to the relationship between David and Kelly and the fact that other Loomis employees believed that they'd dated. This was key information for the FBI, the only clue that David had a possible accomplice, and it ensured that Kelly Campbell's every move would be scrutinized. Even had she fled without a trace, the FBI would've monitored her relatives in case she decided to contact them. Clearly, given her connection to David, there was no way she could have enjoyed her share of the money while living in Gaston County without being discovered.

As for David, while he may have known a few things about the FBI from books, it hadn't occurred to him that agents would do the thorough job they did of investigating him, including pumping his past and current coworkers for information. Had he realized that before the heist, maybe he would have reconsidered Kelly's invite and rejected the whole idea, recruited somebody else on his own, or taken a more manageable load and driven out west.

Steve Chambers too could have sat on the money or at least spent it less quickly and recklessly than he did. But even had he been more cautious, the FBI would've still been watching Kelly, and Steve would've had to keep his distance from her, both in person and over the phone, which—given the critical role Kelly played in getting David Ghantt to commit the crime for them and given their tight preexisting network—would have been difficult to do.

And while pulling this off by himself would've been extremely difficult for David Ghantt, as he'd correctly surmised, the addition of other people began proving burdensome almost immediately after the actual theft. Only weeks later, he was already concerned he might not receive his share of the money, and he soon began to fear for his life. And he wasn't the only one nervous about the future. Kelly Campbell, from the first week, knew the FBI suspected her as an accomplice due to her friendship with Ghantt. And Steve Chambers, up until his arrest, was constantly worried about managing and hiding the $14 million he controlled, increasingly so after November when Jody Calloway made off with the stash from a storage locker.

The irony is that although they succeeded in stealing the money and managed to hold onto it for a bit, none of them seemed to enjoy their stolen riches except in short spurts and through occasional major purchases. All three of them knew, virtually every step of the way, that they weren't in the clear.

Steve Chambers never let me interview him in person, but in 1998 he agreed to answer a small list of general questions for the *Charlotte Observer* that I had submitted to his lawyer in writing. Among other things, I wanted to know what it felt like for him to live in Cramer Mountain. I expected to hear how much fun and luxurious it had been for him, but here's how he answered: "It was not exciting. It was too complicated and wasn't worth it at all. I wish it hadn't happened."

If there was indeed a truly glorious moment for them, it was the evening of October 4, 1997, when it all began. Soon enough, their antics would guarantee them a place in the annals of Dumb Crook History, but for a few hours on that first night, their prospects were full of promise, with little hint of the great anxieties that would dominate the next five months. And the one person who seemed to truly relish this was David Ghantt.

For a few moments, the life he hated finally seemed fixed in his rearview mirror, and what stood ahead, he was sure, was pure bliss, the type most men would never experience because they didn't have what it takes. He had become like the characters in the books he loved so much.

His confidence knew no bounds that evening, in both his abilities and his judgment. In Kelly Campbell he had a partner he loved, a partner he trusted, a partner who had assembled a team that was taking them over the top. He was so sure everything would work out, he had so much faith in teamwork, that he thought nothing of handing off virtually everything he'd stolen to a group of people he'd never even met, and letting Kelly drive him to an airport in South Carolina.

There were glitches that evening—the airport turned out to be closed and there was the near fiasco with the key ring—but they were overcome, and by evening's end there was $14 million—fourteen million dollars!—in their possession. They had managed to commit one of the largest heists in U.S. history.

When David Ghantt finally boarded the bus for Atlanta en route to Mexico, loaded down with twenty-five grand—more money than he'd ever had in his life—he was exuberant over what he'd just done, wondering what was next, a thief escaping into the night, already in over his head.

Acknowledgments

I want to thank the people involved in the theft and its aftermath who trusted me with their stories. I hope they, and the others, feel this book treats them fairly. I also want to thank the investigators and prosecutors who shared their experiences.

Other people worth mentioning, for all sorts of positive reasons, include my fantastic editor Stephanie Bowen of Sourcebooks; my resourceful agent Agnes Birnbaum; Steve Kirk and Carolyn Sakowski of John F. Blair, Publisher; Michaela Hamilton; Philip Gerard; Noell Tin; James Gronquist; Chris Fialko; Ashley Tillman; James Dunbar; Scott Huseby; Cheryl Nuccio; Kevin Ellis; Dr. Philip and Julie Weiss; Judy and David Taylor of Advanced Bonded Warehousing; Steve Gladden; Harold Bender; Joel Bartow; Jackie Taylor; Michael McGee; Tim Hass; Gary Boyd; the Gaston County court clerks; the court clerks at the federal courthouse in Charlotte; Larry Wiley; current and former *Charlotte Observer* reporters and editors including Joe DePriest, Chip Wilson, Carolyn Murray, Cheryl Carpenter, Anna Griffin, and Aileen Soper. I also want to thank the officials at the Mecklenburg County Jail and at the federal prisons in Butner, North Carolina; Alderson, West Virginia; and Estill, South Carolina. Lastly, I want to thank my parents, my brother Eric, and especially my first editor, Stephanie Platzman-Diamant, to whom this book is dedicated.

About the Author

Photo by Gayle Shomer

Jeff Diamant, an award-winning jour-
nalist, covered the second-largest heist in
U.S. history for the *Charlotte Observer*.
He also worked as a reporter for the
Palm Beach Post and *Newark Star Ledger*,
and his writing has appeared in numer-
ous other publications including the
Washington Post, *Toronto Star*, and the
New York Times. A graduate of Yale
College, he researches American reli-
gious history at the City University of New York and has taught
at Lehman College and Rutgers University–Newark. He lives
in Brooklyn.